Table of Contents

Introduction...4
1. Thinking: How to guess a queen 5
   Responding to one notrump openings.
2. Thinking: Fine points of hand evaluation 11
   The Stayman convention and the Gerber convention
3. Thinking: Introduction to counting as declarer 20
   Opening bids of one of a suit
4. Thinking: When to draw trumps 31
   Responding to the opening bid
5. Thinking: Planning your play as declarer 41
   Opener's rebid
6. Thinking: Your defensive strategy;
   signals on defense 50
   Responder's rebid
7. Thinking: Choosing your opening lead 65
   Slam bidding the expert way
8. Thinking: Reconstructing declarer's hand
   on defense...................................78
   Balancing
9. Thinking: Concentration 93
   Strong and weak two-bids; preemptive openings
10. Thinking: Card combinations as declarer 105
    "Loose ends" in the bidding
    Comprehensive Glossary 120
    Scoring at rubber bridge 136
    Chicago scoring 138
    What the proprieties are about 140

Introduction

This workbook will help you get the most from your bridge course. Included is a summary of the material your teacher will present in each lesson, plus quizzes so that you may test your understanding of that material. We believe that if you learn all the things in this workbook you'll be ready to play with anyone at the bridge table!

There is no substitute for actual play as a learning experience; of course, you should try to practice outside of class as much as possible. In addition, you are encouraged to read other books and look at the bridge column in your local newspaper. You cannot become a fine bridge player in just 20 hours of class time.

The potential rewards for those who master this game are very satisfying. You will have a stimulating way of entertaining yourself and a means of making friends wherever you go. If you are more ambitious, there is organized tournament competition that can lead to a World Championship!

Good luck. Enjoy yourself.

THE BRIDGE STUDENT TEXT

VOLUME 2 — FOR INTERMEDIATE PLAYERS

by Randall Baron
and Frank Stewart

Drawings by Jude Goodwin

Published by
Devyn Press, Inc.
Louisville, Kentucky

3343⊀

Dedications

To C.H.
    —F.S.
To Mary, Devyn and Dustin.
    —R.S.B.

Acknowledgments

Grateful thanks to:
Betty Mattison for her patience and typesetting skills;
Pat Houington, Tony Lipka and Henry Francis for their editorial
    assistance;
Izzy Ellis and V.B.I. for their cover photography;
also to Mary Black, Mimi Maier, Bonnie Baron Pollack and
    Debbie Quire.

The student is referred to as "he" to make the text more
readable.

Copyright © 1988 by Devyn Press, Inc.

Printed in the United States of America.

Devyn Press, Inc.
151 Thierman Lane
Louisville, KY 40207

ISBN 0-910791-52-X

Lesson 1

THINKING:
HOW TO GUESS A QUEEN

(1) You are declarer with these cards in 4♡:

♠ A x x x
♡ J 10 x x
◇ K x x
♣ x x

♠ J x
♡ A Q 9 x x
◇ A Q x
♣ K J x

You opened 1♡ after three passes, West overcalled 1♠, North raised to 2♡, you invited game with 3♡, and North went on to 4♡.

West led the ♠K. You won the ace and took a heart finesse, losing to West's king. He cashed his ♠Q and continued with the ♠10. East showed out and you ruffed. You drew the rest of the trumps and led a club from dummy, East playing small. Do you play your ♣K or ♣J?

*FINDING A QUEEN
DOESN'T HAVE
TO MAKE YOUR HEAD SPIN.*

(2) You are declarer with these cards in 5 ◊ :

♠ x x x
♡ K 10 x x
◊ x x x
♣ A x x

♠ J
♡ A J x
◊ K Q J 10 x x x
♣ K x

The bidding went:

West	North	East	South
1 ♠	Pass	Pass	Double
Pass	2 ♡	Pass	4 ◊
Pass	5 ◊	(All Pass)	

West led the ♠ K and continued with the queen, which you ruffed. The ◊ K was won by East's ace and you ruffed the spade return. After drawing the rest of the trumps, how do you attack the heart suit?

SOLUTIONS:

(1) Play the ♣ K. West would have opened the bidding with the ♣ A in addition to his five good spades and his ♡ K.
(2) Finesse West for the ♡ Q. East would have responded to the opening bid with the ♡ Q in addition to the ◊ A.

RESPONDING TO ONE NOTRUMP OPENINGS:

There are various options:

With 0-7 points	PASS with balanced pattern, or BID TWO OF A SUIT (except clubs) with at least five cards in the suit. This is a weak action and partner must pass.
With 8-9 points	RAISE TO 2 NT with balanced pattern.
With 10-14 points	RAISE TO 3 NT with balanced pattern or BID FOUR OF A MAJOR SUIT with a six-card suit.
With 10 points up	BID THREE OF A SUIT with a good five-card suit or longer. This is forcing (to game) and asks partner to support your suit if possible.
With 15-16 points	RAISE to 4 NT with balanced pattern.
With 17-18 points	RAISE TO 6 NT with balanced pattern.
With 19-20 points	RAISE TO 5 NT with balanced pattern. (This bid invites a grand slam. Partner *must* bid at least 6 NT.)
With 21 points up	BID 7 NT.

Responding to a 2 NT or 3 NT opening is based on the same principles. After responder adds his points to the ones opener showed, he can take over and make sure the partnership reaches the proper level. A slight difference is that *any bid by responder over a 2 NT opening is forcing to game.*

QUIZ ON RESPONDING TO NOTRUMP OPENINGS:

Partner opens 1 NT (16-18 balanced). What is your response with:

1.   ♠ K x
     ♡ A x x
     ♢ K Q x x x
     ♣ Q J x

2.   ♠ K x
     ♡ J x x
     ♢ K x x x
     ♣ x x x x

3.   ♠ x x
     ♡ A x x
     ♢ J x x
     ♣ K x x x x

4.   ♠ K Q x
     ♡ A Q x
     ♢ A K x x
     ♣ Q J x

5.   ♠ x x
     ♡ A Q x x x
     ♢ K Q x
     ♣ x x x

6.   ♠ J x
     ♡ x x x
     ♢ A Q x x x
     ♣ K x x

7.   ♠ K Q x
     ♡ A x x
     ♢ K x x x
     ♣ K x x

8.   ♠ x
     ♡ J 10 x x x x
     ♢ A x x
     ♣ K x x

9.   ♠ x x x x x x x
     ♡ x x x
     ♢ x
     ♣ x x x

10.   ♠ A x
     ♡ K x x
     ♢ A Q x x
     ♣ K J x x

11.   ♠ —
     ♡ K x x
     ♢ Q x x x
     ♣ A Q x x x x

12.   ♠ A K x x x
     ♡ x x
     ♢ A J x x
     ♣ K x

13. ♠ A K x
    ♡ K x x
    ◇ K J x x
    ♣ A J x

14. ♠ x
    ♡ Q x x x x
    ◇ J x x x
    ♣ x x x

15. ♠ x
    ♡ A Q x x x x
    ◇ A x x
    ♣ A J x

Partner opens 2 NT (22-24, balanced). What is your response with:

1. ♠ K x x
   ♡ K x x
   ◇ x x x x
   ♣ x x x

2. ♠ K x x
   ♡ A x x
   ◇ Q x x x
   ♣ J x x

3. ♠ x x
   ♡ Q J x x x
   ◇ K x x
   ♣ x x x

4. ♠ A x
   ♡ x x x
   ◇ K J x x
   ♣ K x x x

5. ♠ x x
   ♡ Q x x
   ◇ x x x
   ♣ A x x x x

9

SOLUTIONS TO QUIZ ON RESPONDING TO NOTRUMP OPENINGS:

1. 4 NT
2. Pass
3. 2 NT
4. 7 NT
5. 3♡

6. 3 NT
7. 4 NT
8. 4♡
9. 2♠
10. 6 NT

11. 3♣
12. 3♠
13. 5 NT
14. 2♡
15. 6♡ (or 3♡)

1. 3 NT
2. 4 NT

3. 3♡
4. 6 NT

5. 3NT

YOUR PARTNERSHIP CAN CREATE A MASTERPIECE WITH ACCURATE NOTRUMP BIDDING.

Lesson 2

THINKING:
FINE POINTS OF HAND EVALUATION

The worth of your hand may depend on many factors. The *number* of points you hold is only one of these factors. Good hand evaluation means knowing when the point-count is *not* a totally accurate way of telling how many tricks you can take. Some high cards, for example, may improve or decrease in value as you listen to the bidding.

You may rely on the point-count to provide a preliminary estimate of a hand's value. But do not forget that the point-count is only a way of translating the trick-taking power of your hand into a number that is easy to communicate to your partner in the bidding. Often, during the bidding, you must think in terms of winners, losers and how the play will go in the contract you'd like to bid.

QUIZ ON FINE POINTS OF HAND EVALUATION:

1. You opened 1 ♡ and partner responded 1 NT. To raise to 2 NT, would you rather have:

    (a) ♠ A x x   (b) ♠ A x x
         ♡ A K 9 8 x   ♡ Q J 10 9 8
         ◇ Q J 10   ◇ A K x
         ♣ K x   ♣ K x

2. The opponents bid and raised spades, and your partner overcalled in hearts. Which hand would you prefer to raise him?

(a) ♠ —
   ♡ x x x
   ◊ K x x x x
   ♣ A x x x x

(b) ♠ —
   ♡ x x x x x
   ◊ K x x x
   ♣ A x x x

3. Partner opened 1 ♠, you raised to 2 ♠. Now he tries for game with 3 ♠. To accept, would you prefer:

(a) ♠ Q x x x
   ♡ x x
   ◊ A x x x
   ♣ Q x x

(b) ♠ A x x x
   ♡ x x
   ◊ Q x x x
   ♣ Q x x

4. You open 1 ♣, left-hand opponent overcalls 1 ♡, and partner bids 1 ♠. You rebid 1 NT and are raised to 2 NT. To go on to 3 NT, would you prefer:

(a) ♠ J x
   ♡ A x x
   ◊ K J x x
   ♣ K Q x x

(b) ♠ A x
   ♡ Q J x
   ◊ x x x x
   ♣ A Q J x

5. Your partner opened 1 ♠. Which hand would you prefer?

(a) ♠ A x x x
   ♡ K x x
   ◊ x
   ♣ x x x x x

(b) ♠ A x x x
   ♡ x x x
   ◊ K
   ♣ x x x x x

6. Your partner opened 1 ♠, right-hand opponent bid 2 ◊, you raised to 2 ♠, left-hand opponent came in with 3 ♣. Partner now tried for game with 3 ♡. To accept, which hand would you prefer?

(a) ♠ K x x x   (b) ♠ K x x x
     ♡ Q x   ♡ J x
     ◊ K x x   ◊ Q x x x
     ♣ x x x x   ♣ K x x

7. Which of these two hands do you prefer?

(a) ♠ A Q x x   (b) ♠ K J x x
     ♡ x x   ♡ Q J x
     ◊ x x x   ◊ Q J x
     ♣ A K x x   ♣ Q J x

8. Which of these two hands do you prefer?

(a) ♠ A K J x x   (b) ♠ J x x x x
     ♡ A Q x x   ♡ A x x x
     ◊ x x x   ◊ K Q x
     ♣ x   ♣ A

SOLUTIONS TO QUIZ ON FINE POINTS OF HAND EVALUATION:

1. (b) is the better hand. You prefer to have intermediate cards in your long suit so that the long cards can surely be established.

2. (b) is the better hand. The principle here is that the worth of your short suits depends on how good your support for partner's suit is. On hand (a), your support is so minimal that partner may have a hard time taking advantage of your shortness. A trump opening lead will be damaging; or,

partner may not be able to get off dummy safely after just one spade ruff.

3. (a) is slightly better. The ♠Q in (a) is bound to be a helpful card, with partner known to have spade length. The value of the ♦Q in (b) is unknown.

4. Prefer hand (b). The problem with (a) is that you lack aces, always a worry when the opponents have a long suit they will try to set up against your notrump contract. When you lack aces, your opponents may have the entries to set up the heart suit before you can get *your* tricks established. *Good hand evaluation often means visualizing how the play will go.*

5. (a) is the better hand. *Singleton* honors are of questionable value.

6. (a) is the better hand. The ♦K is well-positioned, behind the diamond bidder, and the ♡Q is a good card. On (b), the ♦Q is probably worthless, and the ♣K, in front of left-hand opponent's club bid, is suspect.

7. (a) is much the better hand, even though both hands contain 13 points in high cards. Note the Quick-Trick structure.

8. (a) is much the better hand — the high cards are located in the longer suits.

THE STAYMAN CONVENTION AND
THE GERBER CONVENTION

A CONVENTION at bridge is a bid that has been assigned an artificial meaning. Knowledgeable players have decided that the bid is more useful when used as a coded message than when used with its natural meaning. The STAYMAN Convention is used by all good bridge players. It is well worth knowing about and adopting. The purpose of STAYMAN is to locate a major suit as trumps after a notrump opening when there is a 4-4 fit. Without STAYMAN, finding such a trump suit would be difficult.

A response to **2♣** to a 1 NT opening says nothing about responder's clubs. It only asks opener if he has *four cards in either major suit*. Opener then answers as follows:

With four spades	— 2♠
With four hearts	— 2♡
With four cards in both majors	— the stronger suit
With no major suit	— 2♢. This is another coded message, unrelated to diamonds. It merely denies a four-card major.

Over a *2 NT* opening bid, a *3♣* response is played as STAYMAN.

Locating a good trump suit with the STAYMAN Convention can be important. Possession of a trump suit makes it easier for declarer to control the play (the opponents cannot establish a long suit against him, as at notrump) and may provide him with some needed extra tricks.

The GERBER Convention is a response of *4♣* to an opening bid in notrump, used to ask partner how many aces he holds. GERBER is necessary because a 4 NT response to 1 NT (or 2 NT) asks partner to go on to 6 NT with a maximum opening and is *not* ace-asking.

The responses to GERBER are as follows:

4♢	— 0 or 4 aces
4♡	— 1 ace
4♠	— 2 aces
4 NT	— 3 aces

Responder may continue with 5♣ to ask for *kings*. Notice that the scheme of responses is different from the one used with the Blackwood Convention. Be careful not to get confused and give the wrong response.

15

Most pairs use 4♣ as an ace-asking bid *only* in responding to a notrump opening.

QUIZ ON USING THE STAYMAN CONVENTION:

I. Partner has opened 1 NT. What is your response with:

1. ♠ K Q x x
   ♡ x x
   ◊ K Q x x
   ♣ x x x

2. ♠ K Q x x
   ♡ K x
   ◊ J x x x
   ♣ x x x

3. ♠ K Q x x
   ♡ x x
   ◊ J x x x
   ♣ x x x

4. ♠ K Q x x x
   ♡ x x
   ◊ A x x
   ♣ Q x x

5. ♠ K Q x x x
   ♡ A x x x
   ◊ x x
   ♣ Q x

6. ♠ 10 x x x
   ♡ Q J x
   ◊ K Q x
   ♣ A x x

7. ♠ Q x x x
   ♡ J x x x
   ◊ J x x x x
   ♣ —

8. ♠ x
   ♡ x x
   ◊ Q x x x
   ♣ J x x x x x

9. ♠ A J x x x
   ♡ x x
   ◊ K x x
   ♣ x x x

10. ♠ A K x x
    ♡ A Q x x
    ◊ K x x
    ♣ x x

11. ♠ A Q x x x
    ♡ x x
    ◊ x x x x
    ♣ x x

12. ♠ A x x x
    ♡ A x x x x
    ◊ x x
    ♣ J x

II. You opened 1 NT, partner responded 2♣, you bid 2◊, he said 2♠. What do you do now, with:

1. ♠ K x x
   ♡ A Q x
   ◊ K Q x x
   ♣ Q x x

2. ♠ K Q x
   ♡ A K x
   ◊ A x x x x
   ♣ x x

3. ♠ K Q x
   ♡ x x
   ◊ A Q x x
   ♣ A K x x

4. ♠ K x
   ♡ Q J x
   ◊ K Q J x x
   ♣ A x x

5. ♠ K x
   ♡ Q J x
   ◊ K Q J x
   ♣ A Q x x

III. You opened 1 NT, partner responded 2♣, you bid 2♠, he bid 2 NT. What do you do now, with:

1. ♠ K Q x x
   ♡ K x x
   ◊ A x x
   ♣ K J x

2. ♠ K Q x x
   ♡ K x x
   ◊ A Q x
   ♣ K J x

3. ♠ K Q x x
   ♡ A Q x x
   ◊ A x
   ♣ J x x

4. ♠ K Q x x
   ♡ A Q x x
   ◊ A x
   ♣ Q J x

17

QUIZ ON USING THE GERBER CONVENTION:

I.   You opened 1 NT and partner responded 4♣. What do you bid with:

1. ♠ K Q x x   2. ♠ A J x
    ♡ A x x   ♡ A 10 x
    ◇ Q x x   ◇ A x x x x
    ♣ A Q x   ♣ A x

II. Partner opens 1 NT. What would you bid with:

1. ♠ K Q J x x   2. ♠ —
    ♡ A   ♡ A K J x x x
    ◇ K Q J x x x   ◇ x x
    ♣ x   ♣ K Q x x x

SOLUTIONS TO QUIZ ON USING THE STAYMAN CONVENTION:

I.   1. 2♣
     2. 2♣
     3. Pass
     4. 3♠   Stayman is not needed here.
     5. 2♣   If partner says 2◇, jump to 3♠.
     6. 3 NT   Most players would avoid using Stayman on this hand because of the lack of distribution and the poor major suit.
     7. 2♣   Plan to pass *any* bid partner makes.
     8. 2♣   Follow up with 3♣, to show a bad hand with long clubs.
     9. 2♣   Bid 2♠ next (unless partner responds 2♠ and you can raise) to show an invitational hand with five spades.
    10. 2♣   Bid slam if you find a suit, or invite slam in notrump.

| 11. | 2♠ | Too weak for Stayman. |
| 12. | 2♣ | |

II.	1.	Pass
	2.	3♠
	3.	4♠
	4.	2 NT
	5.	3 NT

III.	1.	Pass
	2.	3NT
	3.	3♡
	4.	4♡

SOLUTIONS TO QUIZ ON USING
THE GERBER CONVENTION:

| I. | 1. | 4♠ |
| | 2. | 4◊ |

| II. | 1. | 4♣ |
| | 2. | 3♡ | Gerber would be misguided here because you need to know *which* aces partner has, not just how many. The ♠A in partner's hand would be of no use to you. |

TAKE THE MYSTERY OUT OF BIDDING BY USING STAYMAN AND GERBER.

Lesson 3

THINKING:
INTRODUCTION TO COUNTING
AS DECLARER

Quite often, declarer can better determine his proper line of play if he counts the *distribution* of the defenders' hands. This technique is simple in principle: there are 13 cards in each *suit* and 13 cards in each *hand*. If declarer concentrates on the play and observes as the defenders follow suit or discard, he may be able to arrive at a complete count of the distribution. Applying this technique successfully takes a little practice and persistence, but it is worth the effort. Here is an example:

♠ 7 6
♡ A K 5 3
◊ Q 10 7 5
♣ A J 4

♠ J 8 3
♡ 6
◊ A K J 8 4
♣ K 10 7 5

South is declarer in 5 ◊ after West overcalled in spades. The top spades are cashed and West leads a third round. Declarer ruffs this high in dummy, and East shows out. So declarer knows that *West had six spades* and East had two. Trumps are drawn in two rounds. *West had two diamonds.*

Next, declarer should ruff some hearts in his hand. The idea is to find out about the distribution of the heart suit. Suppose South ruffs a third round of hearts, returns to dummy with a trump, and ruffs a fourth heart. Both opponents follow suit the whole time. So *West had four hearts.* Since West began with

20

13 cards, we know therefore that *he had one club.* Declarer can lead a club to dummy's ace and finesse his ♣10 on the return with complete confidence.

If West had shown up with *three* hearts only, declarer would know that he had *two* clubs and East had four clubs. The odds would therefore favor a club finesse against East.

QUIZ ON COUNTING AS DECLARER:

1.
    ♠ Q 9 5 3
    ♡ Q 7 5
    ◊ K 10 6 4
    ♣ K 5

    ♠ A K 10 6 2
    ♡ 8
    ◊ A J 3
    ♣ A Q 6 2

You are declarer in 6♠ after East overcalled in hearts. The opening lead is the ♡J, and you ruff the second heart. You draw trumps, finding that East had three. Next you play the three top clubs and ruff your fourth club in dummy. East follows suit to all four rounds, and West discards a diamond on the fourth club. What is East's distribution? How do you play the diamond suit?

*ANYONE CAN IMPROVE
HIS BRIDGE
BY COUNTING.*

2.
♠ K 10 7 2
♥ Q 7 5
♦ A K 3
♣ A 9 4

♠ A Q 9 6 4 3
♥ 4
♦ 8 6
♣ K 10 7 3

After East opened 3 ♥, you and partner got overboard in 6 ♠. West leads the ♥ A and another heart and you ruff. You draw two rounds of trumps, finding East with two. Next you play the high diamonds and ruff a diamond. Both opponents follow suit. A trump to dummy is followed by a heart ruff, and West discards a diamond. What is East's probable distribution? How do you play the clubs?

3.
♠ 7 6 5
♥ A Q 4
♦ 8 7 4 3
♣ K J 6

♠ K Q J
♥ K 7 2
♦ A K Q J
♣ A 10 4

West leads the ♠ 10 against your 6 NT contract. East wins the ace and returns a spade. When you cash the other high spade, East discards a club. Both opponents follow suit to the three top hearts. You cash the diamonds next, and West follows to four rounds, while East discards the 13th heart and two more clubs. What is West's distribution? What is East's distribution? How do you play the club suit?

4. ♠ K J 7 5
♥ Q 7 5
♦ A 10 5
♣ A K 5

♠ A Q 9 6 4
♥ 9 6 3
♦ K J 8
♣ 7 4

You are declarer in 4 ♠. West cashes the ♡ A and ♡ K, and East shows out on the second round. A third heart is ruffed by East. The ♣ Q is returned and dummy wins. You draw three rounds of trumps, finding that East had only one trump to begin with. Next you play the ♣ A and ♣ K and ruff a club, to which both opponents follow suit. What is West's probable distribution? How do you play the diamond suit?

SOLUTIONS TO QUIZ ON COUNTING AS DECLARER:

1. East showed up with three spades and four clubs, and should have five or more hearts for his overcall. So he had at most one diamond. Cash the ◊ A and lead a diamond to the 10.

2. East had two spades, seven hearts, and at least three diamonds. So he had one club at most. Your only chance is that East had a singleton club *honor*. Cash the ♣ K, and if an honor appears to your right, lead a club to dummy's 9.

3. West had five spades, three hearts, four diamonds, and one club. East had two spades, four hearts, one diamond, and six clubs. Lead a club to the king and a club to your 10.

4. West had six hearts and three spades, and at least three clubs. So he had at most one diamond. Play a diamond to the ace and a diamond to your jack.

OPENING BIDS OF ONE OF A SUIT:

To open the bidding with *one of a suit* you require potential *tricks, defensive* strength and prospects of an easy *rebid.* You will open *almost all* hands that contain *13* high-card points, and you *must* open with *14* high-card points or more. You may well open with slightly *fewer* than 13 high-card points if your hand contains a promising source of tricks.

If you have a *close decision* about whether to open, be influenced by these factors:

1. Your Quick-Trick structure. Quick Tricks are a measure of the *defensive* worth of a hand and are counted according to the following table:

A	= 1	QT
AK in same suit	= 2	QT
AQ in same suit	= 1½	QT
KQ in same suit	= 1	QT
K	= ½	QT

    You prefer that most of your high-card points be concentrated in aces and kings. *Do not open any hand that is sub-minimum in high cards and contains fewer than 2 Quick Tricks.*

2. The *quality of your suits* and the number of tricks they rate to produce.

3. Your *spot cards.* Tens, nines and eights are valuable cards, especially if the play is at notrump.

4. Your holding in the *major suits,* especially *spades.* With length in the ranking suits, you can outbid the opponents if the auction turns competitive, so you are more willing to open.

5. The ease with which you can *rebid.* A potentially uncomfortable rebid problem may influence you *not* to open on a borderline hand.

Once you have decided that your hand is worth an opening bid, you must choose a suit. There are simple guidelines:

WITH ONE LONG SUIT — open one of that suit. (Minor suits only four cards long are often opened.)

WITH TWO LONG SUITS (five cards or more in each one) — usually open the higher-ranking suit. (With five clubs and five spades, usually open 1♣.)

WITH TWO FOUR-CARD MINOR SUITS — open 1♣*.

NOTE WELL: WITH ONE FOUR-CARD MINOR SUIT and no longer suit, open in the minor. AVOID OPENING IN A FOUR-CARD MAJOR SUIT (unless your suit is so strong that you would welcome a raise with only three cards).

Since most players promise at least a five-card suit when they open in a major suit, you are often obliged to open a good three-card minor suit (clubs, unless your distribution is precisely 4-4-3-2). The alternative, opening a four-card major, is worse. Many players call this bid the "short club," but "prepared bid" is more accurate. One advantage of this opening is that it starts the auction low and allows you to keep another suit in reserve for a rebid.

----

*If balanced, you plan to rebid in notrump. However, with very strong diamonds, or with two four-card minors so strong that you will treat your hand as a two-suiter and show both suits, a 1 ◊ opening is preferable.

Also, some hands with *three* four-card suits require special treatment. If you have 1-4-4-4 distribution, a 1♠ response to 1♣ would leave you without a good rebid; with 4-1-4-4 distribution a 1 NT response to a 1♣ opening would be awkward. In both cases, therefore tend to open 1 ◊.

For further explanation, see the material on opener's rebid, especially the discussion of *reverses*.

QUIZ ON OPENING ONE OF A SUIT:

Decide whether each of these hands is an opening bid and, if so, in what suit you should open.

1. ♠ K x
   ♡ Q J x x
   ◇ K J x x
   ♣ Q J x

2. ♠ K
   ♡ A J x
   ◇ K x x x
   ♣ J x x x x

3. ♠ A Q x x x x
   ♡ A J x
   ◇ x x
   ♣ x x

4. ♠ A x x x
   ♡ Q x x
   ◇ Q x x
   ♣ A x x

5. ♠ A K x x
   ♡ x x
   ◇ x x x
   ♣ A J x x

6. ♠ A 10 9 x
   ♡ x x
   ◇ A J 10 x
   ♣ K 10 x

7. ♠ A J 10 x x
   ♡ A J 10 x x
   ◇ Q x
   ♣ x

8. ♠ A J x x x x x
   ♡ A J x x
   ◇ x
   ♣ x

9. ♠ A
   ♡ Q x
   ◇ Q x x x x
   ♣ K x x x x

10. ♠ A Q 10 x
    ♡ x x x
    ◇ A Q x x
    ♣ x x

11. ♠ A K Q x x x
    ♡ K x
    ◇ x x
    ♣ x x x

12. ♠ A K
    ♡ K x
    ◇ x x x
    ♣ Q J x x x x

13. ♠ A K x
    ♡ K x x
    ◇ x x x
    ♣ Q J x x

14. ♠ A K x
    ♡ x x x
    ◇ A Q x
    ♣ J x x x

15. ♠ A K x
    ♡ x x x
    ◇ J x x x
    ♣ A Q x

16. ♠ J x x x x
    ♡ A K x x
    ◇ A Q x
    ♣ x

17. ♠ A K Q
    ♡ J x x x x
    ◇ —
    ♣ K x x x x

18. ♠ A K x x
    ♡ x x x
    ◇ J x
    ♣ A J x x

19. ♠ A x
    ♡ K Q x x
    ◇ A J x x
    ♣ x x x

20. ♠ x x
    ♡ A x x
    ◇ A Q x x
    ♣ K J x x

21. ♠ x x
    ♡ A K x x
    ◇ Q x x
    ♣ K J x x

22. ♠ x x
    ♡ A K J x
    ◇ J x x
    ♣ Q J x x

23. ♠ K J x x
    ♡ A x x x
    ◇ x
    ♣ A J x x

24. ♠ K J x x
    ♡ x
    ◇ A J x x
    ♣ K Q x x

25. ♠ J x x x
    ♡ A J x x
    ◇ A K x x
    ♣ x

26. ♠ A J x x
    ♡ x
    ◇ x x x x
    ♣ A K J 10

27. ♠ x x
    ♡ x x x
    ◊ A K J x
    ♣ A K J 10

28. ♠ A x x x
    ♡ x x x
    ◊ K x x
    ♣ A Q x

29. ♠ K x x x
    ♡ Q x x x
    ◊ J x
    ♣ A K x

30. ♠ J x x x
    ♡ Q x x x
    ◊ A K x
    ♣ A x

31. ♠ A Q x
    ♡ A K J 10
    ◊ x x x
    ♣ x x x

32. ♠ A J x x x
    ♡ A K x x x
    ◊ x x
    ♣ x

33. ♠ x
    ♡ A Q x x x
    ◊ K x
    ♣ A J x x x

34. ♠ Q x
    ♡ A Q x x x
    ◊ K J x
    ♣ A 10 x

35. ♠ A K x x
    ♡ x x
    ◊ A K Q x
    ♣ K x x

36. ♠ A K J x x
    ♡ K Q x x
    ◊ x
    ♣ A J x

37. ♠ x
    ♡ A K x x
    ◊ A Q J x
    ♣ A Q x x

38. ♠ Q x x x x
    ♡ A x
    ◊ x
    ♣ A Q J x x

39. ♠ A x
    ♡ K Q x x x
    ◊ Q J x x x x
    ♣ —

40. ♠ A Q x x x
    ♡ A K J x x
    ◊ A x
    ♣ x

SOLUTIONS TO QUIZ ON OPENING ONE OF A SUIT:

1. Pass; lacking in defensive strength.
2. Pass; bad suits, poor defense, rebid problems.
3. 1♠.
4. Pass; too many losers.
5. 1♣.
6. 1◊; good spot cards.
7. 1♠.
8. 1♠; winners, defensive tricks, an easy second bid.
9. Pass; bad suits.
10. 1◊; *3* Quick Tricks.
11. 1♠.
12. 1♣.
13. 1♣.
14. 1♣.
15. 1◊.
16. 1♠.
17. 1♡.
18. 1♣.
19. 1◊.
20. 1♣.
21. 1♣.
22. Pass; this is a borderline hand — an opening bid of 1♣ certainly could not be criticized.
23. 1♣.
24. 1◊. 1♣ would cause rebid problems over 1 NT.
25. 1◊.
26. 1♣. Diamonds are weak, clubs are strong.
27. 1◊; treating this hand as a two-suiter and planning to bid both suits.
28. 1♣.
29. 1♣.
30. 1◊.
31. 1♡.
32. 1♠.

33. 1♡.
34. 1 NT; this is a balanced 16-count.
35. 1◇.
36. 1♠.
37. 1◇; some very strong hands must be opened with a bid of just *one* of a suit.
38. 1♣; an exception to our rule of handling two long suits.
39. 1♡; another exceptional case; with this minimum hand, you should be interested in *economy*.
40. 1♠; don't make the mistake of opening 1♡, planning to "reverse" into spades. Open 1♠, *jump in hearts*.

KNOWING THE CORRECT OPENING BID IS
SWEET MUSIC TO YOUR PARTNER'S EARS.

Lesson 4

THINKING: WHEN TO DRAW TRUMPS

On most hands, declarer will try to *draw the opponents' trumps* as soon as he can so he can cash his other winners safely. There are, however, a variety of circumstances in which declarer *cannot do this immediately:*

1. When he needs to *ruff some losers* with dummy's trumps.
2. When he needs to ruff cards in his own hand in playing a *dummy reversal.*
3. When he plays a *cross-ruff.* In this type of play, declarer will *never* draw trumps at all.
4. When he needs *entries* that only the trump suit can provide.
5. When there are *timing* problems and he has something more important to do first (for instance, the establishment of a quick discard for an impending loser.)
6. When he needs to *keep control* of the play and must establish a side suit before playing trumps.
7. *In some hands,* when the opponents remain with a single *high* trump. Declarer may establish and cash winners in the other suits, ignoring the sure trump trick the opponents have.

In contrast, the time when you do want to draw trumps is when you have plenty of winners, with every suit under control, and there is nothing to do but draw trumps and cash your winners.

> DRAW TRUMPS IMMEDIATELY *ONLY* IF THE HAND PRESENTS *NO PROBLEMS* WHATEVER. IF YOU SEE A REASON *NOT* TO DRAW THE TRUMPS IMMEDIATELY, *WAIT* UNTIL THE PROPER TIME.

QUIZ ON DRAWING TRUMPS:

1. ♠ A K
    ♡ A Q J 10
    ◇ 4 3 2
    ♣ Q 10 8 7

    ♠ 4 3
    ♡ 5 4 3
    ◇ K 7 6
    ♣ A K J 3 2

    Contract: 5♣
    Opening lead: ♠Q
    Plan the play.

2. ♠ Q J
    ♡ J 9 4 2
    ◇ A 4 3
    ♣ 6 5 4 3

    ♠ A 10 5
    ♡ A Q 10 6 5
    ◇ K 6 5
    ♣ K Q

    Contract: 4♡
    Opening lead: ◇Q
    Plan the play.

*WHEN YOU ARE DECLARER,
IT IS IMPORTANT TO
KNOW WHEN TO DRAW
TRUMPS AND
WHEN TO WAIT.*

3. ♠ 3 2
   ♥ A K Q J 10
   ♦ 2
   ♣ A 7 6 5 4

   ♠ A K 8 7 6 5
   ♥ 3 2
   ♦ A 8 7 6
   ♣ 8

   Contract: 6♠
   Opening lead: ♦ K
   Plan the play.

4. ♠ J 5
   ♥ Q 7 6 5 4
   ♦ Q 10 4 3
   ♣ Q 3

   ♠ A K Q 10 9 4
   ♥ K 2
   ♦ K J 7 5
   ♣ J

   Contract: 4♠
   Opening lead: ♣ 2
   The ace wins to
   your right and a
   club is returned.
   Plan the play.

SOLUTIONS TO QUIZ ON DRAWING TRUMPS:

1. Declarer may need to finesse in hearts *three* times so he must be careful with his entries to hand. He plays a trump to the jack and finesses in hearts; then queen of trumps, a trump to the ace, and another heart finesse; finally, a trump to the king for another heart finesse, if necessary.

2. Declarer has a potential loser in each suit, but he can *discard a diamond from dummy on a spade.* He should win the opening lead in dummy and make a spade play *immediately,* setting up his pitch. If he takes a (losing) trump finesse at trick two, the defenders will get to lead diamonds again, setting up their winner, and declarer will have "lost a tempo" and maybe his contract.

3. Declarer's best play is to win the ♦ A and *duck a round of trumps.* He can win whatever the opponents lead next, draw two more rounds of trumps (hopefully all of them) and run his winners without fear the opponents will ruff in. There are potential problems on any other line of play.

4. If declarer ruffs the second club and draws trumps, he will be in trouble if trumps split 4-1. He will have only *one* trump left and must knock out *two* aces to come to ten tricks. The opponents will lead clubs at every opportunity and declarer will *lose control.* Declarer should instead lead *a low heart at trick two.* If he wins this trick, he can draw trumps (even if they are 4-1) and knock out the ◊ A for ten tricks.

Even if the opponents win the first heart, they cannot force declarer in clubs because dummy is *also* void and still has some trumps. (It is true that declarer might run into a diamond ruff if he does not draw trumps right away; but the opponents did not try for a diamond ruff when they had the chance. A 4-1 trump break is a bigger danger.)

RESPONDING TO THE OPENING BID:

With 6 points or more, RESPOND if partner opens the bidding with one of a suit. You should respond, even with a poorish hand, because partner could have *20* points or even more, and game is possible even if you are weak. Also, the suit partner suggests as trumps with his first bid may not be the best one available. You may wish to suggest another suit. You are especially interested in finding a *major* suit for trumps if you have a fit there.

While you may be obliged to respond with weakness, you may also choose to respond with a *minimum* bid even if your hand is fairly *strong.* The purpose of this is to save bidding room so you and partner can exchange as much information as possible and decide on an accurate contract.

Responder has several options at his first turn. They fall into three categories:

RAISE partner's suit to two with 6-9 points and four-card support or better. (It is permissible to raise a *major*-suit opening to *two* with only *three*-card support.

RAISE partner's suit to three with 13-15 points and good four-card support or better. This bid is *forcing*. Partner must continue at least to game.

RAISE partner's suit straight to game with excellent support and a distributional hand, but fewer than 10 high-card points. This bid is primarily intended to keep the opponents from bidding.

BID A NEW SUIT at the one level with 6 points or more.

BID A NEW SUIT at the two level with 10 points or more. Responder may bid *any* suit* of four or more cards, merely suggesting a trump suit. Any new suit bid by responder is *forcing* — you may choose to respond as cheaply as possible even with a sound hand in order to conserve bidding space. Therefore . . .

JUMP IN A NEW SUIT only with a good suit and a very powerful hand. This is a way responder can alert his partner that slam is possible.

BID 1 NT with 6-9 points, no support for your partner's suit, and no suit that you could show at the one level.

BID 2 NT with 13-15 points, balanced pattern, and a "stopper" in all the unbid suits. This bid is *forcing*.

BID 3 NT with 16-18 points and balanced pattern.

Rarely, responder may choose a *preemptive* response. If the opening bid, for example, is 1 ◇, responses of *4 ◇* or *three of a major suit* would be *preemptive*.

———
*The only exception is that a 2 ♡ response to a 1 ♠ opening suggests five or more hearts.

QUIZ ON RESPONDING TO SUIT OPENINGS:

I. Partner has opened 1 ♠. Give the correct response with:

1. ♠ J x x
   ♡ Q x
   ◊ Q x x x
   ♣ x x x x

2. ♠ J x x x
   ♡ x x
   ◊ A Q x x
   ♣ x x x

3. ♠ J x x
   ♡ x x
   ◊ A Q x x x
   ♣ x x x

4. ♠ A K x x
   ♡ x x
   ◊ A x x x
   ♣ Q x x

5. ♠ Q J x x x
   ♡ —
   ◊ Q 10 x x x x
   ♣ x x

6. ♠ x x
   ♡ K Q x x x
   ◊ x x x
   ♣ K x x

7. ♠ x
   ♡ K x x
   ◊ x x x
   ♣ K J x x x x

8. ♠ x x
   ♡ A J x x
   ◊ K Q x
   ♣ K J x x

9. ♠ Q x x
   ♡ K x x
   ◊ A Q x x
   ♣ A J x

10. ♠ x x
    ♡ A K x
    ◊ x x x
    ♣ K J x x x

11. ♠ A K x x
    ♡ x
    ◊ A x x
    ♣ K Q 10 x x

12. ♠ x
    ♡ A Q x x
    ◊ A K x
    ♣ K Q x x x

13. ♠ x
    ♡ K x x x
    ◇ A Q x x
    ♣ A x x x

14. ♠ Q x x x
    ♡ x x
    ◇ A K J x
    ♣ x x x

15. ♠ A Q x x
    ♡ x x
    ◇ A K J 10 x
    ♣ x x

II. Partner has opened 1 ◇ . Give the correct response with:

1. ♠ x x
    ♡ A K
    ◇ J x x x x
    ♣ x x x x

2. ♠ x x
    ♡ A x x
    ◇ A Q x x x
    ♣ K x x

3. ♠ K J x x
    ♡ Q x x
    ◇ x x x
    ♣ x x x

4. ♠ A K x x x
    ♡ A x x
    ◇ K x x
    ♣ x x

5. ♠ A J x x
    ♡ Q x x x
    ◇ x x
    ♣ J x x

6. ♠ A x x x x
    ♡ Q J x x x
    ◇ x
    ♣ A x

7. ♠ A K J x
    ♡ K Q 10 x
    ◇ x x
    ♣ x x x

8. ♠ Q x x
    ♡ K x x
    ◇ A x x
    ♣ x x x x

9. ♠ K J x
    ♡ A 10 x
    ◇ J x x
    ♣ K Q x x

10. ♠ K J x
    ♡ A 10 x
    ◇ J x x x
    ♣ K Q x

11. ♠ A Q x
   ♡ K Q x
   ◊ J x x
   ♣ K Q x x

12. ♠ K J x
   ♡ A Q x x
   ◊ x x
   ♣ K x x x

13. ♠ A K J x x
   ♡ A x
   ◊ A J x x
   ♣ x x

14. ♠ A Q x x
   ♡ A K x x
   ◊ x
   ♣ A J x x

15. ♠ —
   ♡ x x x
   ◊ K Q 10 x x x
   ♣ J 10 x x

III. With each of these hands, give the correct response to an opening bid in each of the four suits:

1. ♠ x
   ♡ K 10 x x x x
   ◊ Q J x
   ♣ J x x

2. ♠ x x
   ♡ A J x x
   ◊ K Q x x
   ♣ K 10 x

3. ♠ x x
   ♡ A Q x x
   ◊ x x x
   ♣ A K x x

4. ♠ A x
   ♡ K x x x
   ◊ x x x
   ♣ K J x x

5. ♠ A K
   ♡ J x x x
   ◊ 10 x x x
   ♣ x x x

SOLUTIONS TO QUIZ ON RESPONDING TO SUIT OPENINGS:

I.   1. Pass
     2. 2♠
     3. 2♠
     4. 3♠
     5. 4♠
     6. 1 NT
     7. 1 NT   (no choice)
     8. 2 NT
     9. 3 NT
   10. 2♣
   11. 3♣   (planning to support spades next)
   12. 2♣   (save room to find your best strain)
   13. 2♣   (avoid a 2 NT response with unbalanced pattern)
   14. 2◇   (you must temporize)
   15. 2◇   (you may show a *very strong side* suit even when a double raise of partner's suit is possible)

II.   1. 2◇
     2. 3◇
     3. 1♠
     4. 1♠
     5. 1♡   (show four-card majors "up-the-line")
     6. 1♠
     7. 1♠   (an exception; since these suits are so strong, you should treat them as long suits and plan to bid both of them)
     8. 1 NT
     9. 2 NT
   10. 2 NT   (more descriptive than a diamond raise)
   11. 3 NT
   12. 1♡
   13. 2♠

14. 1 ♡   (save room because the best trump suit is in doubt)

15. 4 ◇   (but the vulnerability must be considered before making this bid)

III. 1.   1 ♠ - 1 NT   2.   1 ♠ - 2 NT
       1 ♡ - 4 ♡   1 ♡ - 3 ♡
       1 ◇ - 1 ♡   1 ◇ - 1 ♡
       1 ♣ - 1 ♡   1 ♣ - 1 ♡

   3.   1 ♠ - 2 ♣   4.   1 ♠ - 2 ♣
       1 ♡ - 3 ♡   1 ♡ - 2 ♣
       1 ◇ - 1 ♡   1 ◇ - 1 ♡
       1 ♣ - 1 ♡   1 ♣ - 1 ♡

   5.   1 ♠ - 1 NT
       1 ♡ - 2 ♡
       1 ◇ - 1 ♡
       1 ♣ - 1 ♡

BRIDGE IS AN EASY GAME
WHEN YOU BID WELL!

Lesson 5

THINKING: PLANNING YOUR PLAY
AS DECLARER

Since hasty play to the first trick is a common error, a good declarer must do some thinking and planning before he touches a single card. The most important step in your planning is *counting* your sure *winners* and potential *losers*.

At NOTRUMP . . .	Always count your sure *winners*.
In a SUIT CONTRACT . . .	Count your potential *losers* if the contract is a fairly *high*-level one (at game or higher). You will usually have only a few losers and it should be easier to count *them*. If the contract is a low partscore, it may be easier for you to count what *winners* you have.
On MANY HANDS . . .	You will do well to count *both* winners and losers.

This counting tells you how many extra winners you must develop or how many losers you must avoid. There are many ways, as we have seen, to establish tricks: you may set up long cards or intermediates, take finesses, or make extra tricks in the trump suit. But . . .

YOU MUST HAVE A PLAN AND YOU MUST DECIDE EARLY WHAT IT WILL BE.

QUIZ ON PLANNING THE PLAY AS DECLARER:

1. ♠ 6 5 4 3
   ♥ A 9
   ♦ Q 5 4
   ♣ 7 6 5 4

   ♠ A K Q
   ♥ J 4
   ♦ A K 3 2
   ♣ A Q 8 2

   Contract: 3 NT
   Opening lead: ♥7
   Plan the play.

2. ♠ Q J 2
   ♥ 4 3 2
   ♦ A 7 6 5 4
   ♣ A Q

   ♠ A K 10 9 7 3
   ♥ A 8 7
   ♦ 8 3
   ♣ 5 4

   Contract: 4♠
   Opening lead: ♣2
   Plan the play.

3. ♠ 4 3
   ♥ K J 5
   ♦ J 6 5
   ♣ A Q 7 5 4

   ♠ A 10 2
   ♥ A Q 10 7 3
   ♦ 8 3 2
   ♣ K 8

   Contract: 4♥
   Opening lead: ♦A

The opponents cash three diamond tricks and shift to a spade. Plan the play.

SOLUTIONS TO QUIZ ON PLANNING
THE PLAY AS DECLARER:

1. Declarer has eight top tricks and many chances for a ninth.
    He should plan the play so he can try *every* possible chance.
    He ducks the opening lead, in case West has led from a
    heart suit headed by the king-queen. Assuming East wins
    and returns a heart, declarer wins and tests spades. If the
    suit splits 3-3, the ◊ Q is an entry to the long card.

    If spades fail to break, declarer tries diamonds next.
    He cashes three rounds *ending in dummy.* If the suit splits
    3-3, declarer plays a club to his ace and takes his good
    diamond.

    If diamonds fail to split, declarer must fall back on the
    club finesse as his last chance, and the lead is in dummy
    so he can lead a club to his queen. (The club play should
    be the last resort, since the defenders will cash hearts if
    they get in. It costs declarer nothing, however, to test the
    spades and diamonds.)

2. Declarer should *win the* ♣*A* and rely on diamonds. A los-
    ing club finesse at trick one will lead to a certain set when
    the defenders switch to hearts.

    Declarer chances of setting up a diamond trick are ex-
    cellent. He ducks a diamond at trick two to keep all his
    entries to dummy available. The defense will win, cash
    the ♣K, and lead a heart. Declarer wins, plays ◊ A, ruffs
    a diamond with a high trump, leads a trump to dummy
    and ruffs another diamond high. The fifth diamond in dum-
    my will be a winner now, even if an opponent began with
    four diamonds.

    Declarer now draws two more rounds of trumps, *end-
    ing in dummy,* and cashes his good diamond. (If diamonds
    split 3-3, only one diamond needs to be ruffed and declarer
    makes an overtrick.)

3. If trumps split 3-2, declarer can afford to ruff a club (high) in his hand to cater to a 4-2 club break. If trumps are 4-1, declarer must hope clubs split 3-3, since he cannot ruff a club and draw trumps ending in dummy. Since all depends on the trump suit, declarer should test it first by playing the ace and jack. If trumps are 4-1, declarer draws all the trumps and plays three high clubs. If both defenders follow to two trumps, the play continues: ♣K, ♣A, club ruff high, ♡K, ♣Q, club.

OPENER'S REBID

There are several options:

CASE ONE — *If responder has made a bid that limits his strength:*

PASS —	if you know that no game contract is possible and you are satisfied with the contract.
TRY TO IMPROVE THE CONTRACT —	if partner responds 1 NT, suggest another suit if your hand looks unsuitable for notrump.
TRY FOR GAME—	if responder has limited his hand and there may be a game depending on whether he is minimum or maximum for his bidding.
FORCE TO GAME —	by jumping in a new suit.
BID GAME —	if you know the values for game are present and which game contract is best.

CASE TWO — *If responder bids a new suit:* opener must describe his hand further —

REBID THE MINIMUM NUMBER OF NOTRUMP — with 13-15 points and balanced pattern. This bid denies another suit you could show at the one level as well as four-card support for partner's suit.
JUMP ONE LEVEL IN NOTRUMP — with 19-20 points and balanced pattern. With a balanced 21 points, you would jump all the way to 3 NT.

RAISE PARTNER'S SUIT ONE LEVEL — with 13-15 points and four-card support (rarely, three-card support).
RAISE PARTNER'S SUIT TWO LEVELS — with 16-18 points and four-card support.
RAISE PARTNER'S SUIT TO GAME — with 19-20 points and four-card support.

If you hold a second suit of four or more cards —
BID YOUR SECOND SUIT — as cheaply as possible with 13-18 points.*
JUMP IN YOUR SECOND SUIT — with 19 points or more. This bid, a jump shift, is forcing (to game).

If you hold just one long suit —
REBID YOUR LONG SUIT — as cheaply as possible with 13-15 points.
JUMP IN YOUR LONG SUIT — with 16-18 points. This bid would suggest a good six- or seven-card suit.

---

*See, however, the material in REVERSES, starting on the next page.

In theory, you may REBID any suit of five or more cards. Avoid doing so, however, if there is an alternative. Rebid in notrump if your hand is balanced or show another suit if you have one.

NOTE THIS WELL! In an auction like:

Opener	Responder
1 ♣	1 ♠
2 ◊	

responder, if he wishes to (or must) take a *preference* to the first suit opener offered, must do so at the level of *three*. Opener's bidding, in effect, says he feels a nine-trick contract will be safe if responder prefers his first suit. This is an example of a REVERSE by opener (so called because he has *reversed* the usual order of showing the suits in a two-suited hand, higher-ranking first).

REVERSES show extra strength. About 17 high-card points or more (a trick better than a minimum opening) is needed. In addition, a reverse always promises a two-suited hand with *greater length in the first suit.*

If you open 1 ◊ on:

> ♠ x x
> ♡ K Q x x
> ◊ A J x x
> ♣ A x x

and partner responds 1 ♠, *rebid 1 NT,* showing a balanced minimum, *not* 2 ♡, a reverse that might land you too high.

46

QUIZ ON OPENER'S REBID:

I. You opened 1♠, partner responded 2◊. What is your rebid?

1. ♠ A K Q x x
   ♡ A x x
   ◊ x x
   ♣ x x x

2. ♠ A Q x x x
   ♡ K x x
   ◊ J x
   ♣ K J x

3. ♠ A Q J x x
   ♡ K J x x
   ◊ x
   ♣ Q x x

4. ♠ A J 10 x x
   ♡ A K
   ◊ x
   ♣ Q x x x x

5. ♠ A Q J x x x
   ♡ A x x
   ◊ A x
   ♣ Q x

II. You opened 1♡, partner responded 2♡. What is your rebid?

1. ♠ A Q
   ♡ A J x x x
   ◊ K Q x
   ♣ K J x

2. ♠ A x
   ♡ A J x x x
   ◊ A Q x x
   ♣ K x

3. ♠ A x
   ♡ A K J x x
   ◊ A x x
   ♣ x x x

III. You opened 1♣, partner responded 1♡. What is your rebid?

1. ♠ Q x x
   ♡ x x
   ◊ A K x x
   ♣ A J x x

2. ♠ A Q J x
   ♡ x x
   ◊ A x
   ♣ A J x x x

47

3. ♠ A x
   ♥ x x
   ♦ A K J x
   ♣ A Q x x x

4. ♠ A x
   ♥ x x
   ♦ Q x x x
   ♣ A K J x x

5. ♠ x x
   ♥ K x x x
   ♦ A x
   ♣ A Q x x x

6. ♠ x
   ♥ K x x
   ♦ A x x
   ♣ A K Q x x x

7. ♠ x x
   ♥ A K x x
   ♦ Q x
   ♣ A K x x x

8. ♠ x x
   ♥ A Q x x
   ♦ A x x
   ♣ A K Q x

9. ♠ A J x
   ♥ K x x
   ♦ K x x
   ♣ A K J x

10. ♠ A K J x
    ♥ x x
    ♦ A x
    ♣ A K x x x

IV. You opened 1♠, partner responded 1 NT. What is your rebid?

1. ♠ A K J x x x
   ♥ Q x x x
   ♦ K x
   ♣ x

2. ♠ A K Q x x x
   ♥ Q x
   ♦ K x x
   ♣ Q x

3. ♠ A Q x x x
   ♥ A x x
   ♦ x
   ♣ K J x x

4. ♠ A K J x x
   ♥ A x x
   ♦ x
   ♣ A Q J x

5. ♠ K J x x x
   ♥ A x x
   ♦ A x
   ♣ Q x x

48

SOLUTIONS TO QUIZ ON OPENER'S REBID:

I. 1. 2♠
    2. 2 NT (showing a balanced minimum)
    3. 2♡
    4. 2♠   (3♣ would be a reverse, promising more in high cards)
    5. 3♠
II. 1. 3 NT (partner can always return to hearts if his hand is unbalanced)
    2. 4♡
    3. 3♡
III. 1. 1 NT (*not* 2♦, which would be a reverse)
     2. 1♠
     3. 2♦   (you have adequate strength for a reverse)
     4. 2♣   (you would prefer another club, but there is no choice)
     5. 2♡
     6. 3♣
     7. 3♡
     8. 4♡
     9. 2 NT
    10. 2♠
IV. 1. 2♠
    2. 2 NT (3♠ is possible, but this hand is notrump-oriented)
    3. 2♣
    4. 3♣
    5. Pass

Lesson 6

THINKING: YOUR DEFENSIVE STRATEGY; SIGNALS ON DEFENSE

While basic defensive rules such as LEAD THROUGH STRENGTH, UP TO WEAKNESS are often sufficient to handle problems on defense, at times you must judge for yourself what suit to lead, and common sense may suggest that you break the rule. Here are some situations when you may judge the need to lead a specific suit:

1. If the dummy is *very strong* and will provide declarer with several *discards* for his losers, you must try to set up a *fast trick* in the most likely suit, even if it means *taking a chance* (by leading away from an honor).
2. If the dummy is very weak, without much help for declarer, he will have *inevitable* losers. The defenders can afford to *wait* for their tricks. Lead a *safe* suit (perhaps a trump), one in which you cannot give away a trick.
3. If the dummy has *ruffing power,* consider leading a *trump.*
4. A suit in which your partner has opened the bidding or overcalled usually makes a desirable suit to lead.
5. A *sequential* holding, such as Q-J-10-x, is always a lead to consider because it is *safe* and begins to *build a trick* in the suit as well.

QUIZ ON YOUR DEFENSIVE STRATEGY:

1.
     ♠ 7 6 4
     ♡ J 10
     ◊ A K 5 4
     ♣ 8 6 4 3

♠ Q 8 3
♡ 7 4 3
◊ Q J 10 8
♣ J 7 5

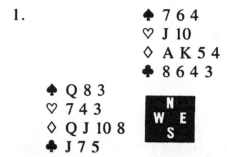

South opened 1♡, North responded 1 NT, South jumped to 4♡, all passed. You lead the ◊Q. Declarer wins the ace and cashes the king, discarding a low club. He then leads a spade to his ten and your queen. What do you lead at this point?

2.
     ♠ 7
     ♡ A J 8 4
     ◊ 8 5 3
     ♣ A Q J 10 3

♠ A Q 8 5
♡ 7 2
◊ K 10 4
♣ 7 6 5 4

North opened 1♣, South responded 1♡, North raised to 2♡, South went to 4♡. You lead the ♠A, winning the first trick. Upon seeing dummy, what do you lead next?

3.   ♠ 10 6 4 2
                    ♡ J 8 5 3
                    ♢ 5
                    ♣ A J 6 4

♠ A K 5
♡ 10 9 7 4
♢ Q 10 7 3
♣ 8 3

South opened 1 ♢, North responded 1 ♡, South rebid 2 ♣, and all passed. You lead the ♠A, winning the first trick. What should you lead at trick two?

SOLUTIONS TO QUIZ ON YOUR DEFENSIVE STRATEGY:

1.   While your side may have tricks available in spades or clubs, there is no hurry to take them — dummy is now worthless, so how can declarer avoid any of his losers? Lead a diamond, forcing declarer to spend a trump (a trick he will always get anyway). By exiting safely, you give nothing away. Leading any other suit may cost a trick by giving declarer a "free finesse."

2.   Here, dummy has teeth. Sooner or later, declarer will draw trumps, establish the clubs (if he doesn't have the ♣K), and discard his diamond losers. You can't afford to defend passively this time. Shift to a low diamond, hoping partner will produce the ace or at least the queen, allowing you to cash or establish some tricks before it's too late.

3.   Dummy has very little in high cards but does contain some trumps and a singleton diamond. Clearly, declarer can use dummy only by ruffing some diamonds, and you can tell he will need to do just that since your diamonds are fairly strong. Shift to a trump at trick two.

On many occasions, your *partner* will *help* you decide what to lead (or whether you should *continue* to lead a suit). He can *signal* you by means of the card he plays. There are several types of defensive signals, but since the defenders' main problem is what suits they should lead or continue leading, the ATTITUDE signal is the most important one. When your partner leads a suit (for example, when he lays down an ace), you should tell him whether this is a good suit to lead again. You play:

YOUR *HIGHEST* AVAILABLE SPOT TO *ENCOURAGE* A CONTINUATION.
YOUR *LOWEST* SPOT TO SHOW *NO* INTEREST AND SUGGEST A *SWITCH*.

For example, if your partner leads the ♡A and your holding is K-Q-9-5-2, you probably would play the *nine,* an encouraging card. With 9-5-2, you would play the *two,* showing no interest in this suit. Sometimes, you will not have a chance to show your ATTITUDE about partner's lead because you will have to play "third hand-high." But if you can show your ATTITUDE, you must do so.

You can also show your ATTITUDE about a suit as you *discard* from it. If declarer is drawing trumps and you wish to discard from ♡KQ853, you would discard the *eight,* suggesting strength in this suit. Partner will know that hearts is a good suit (or at least, a safe suit) to lead.

More about signals:

1. It is not improper to send partner a message merely by using the *card you play* as a signal. It *is* improper, however, to play your cards with a special emphasis. Some people like to slap their encouraging signals on the table with a thump, just to make sure partner notices the signal. This is unethical.

2. The size of the spot cards is *relative*. A *four* may be encouraging if played from A-K-4-2, while an *eight* may be partner's lowest if he has 10-9-8. If your partner plays a card you think is a signal, you must look at your *own* spots, *declarer's* card and the spots in *dummy* and try to decide if partner has played an encouraging or discouraging card.

3. *Declarer* can also see your signals. *Beware* of signaling if the information may be of more use to declarer than to your partner. Signal only if you think your partner needs the information.

QUIZ ON DEFENSIVE SIGNALS:

I. Partner has led the ♠4 against the opponents' contract of 3 NT. Dummy has A-8-5, and declarer plays the ace. What would you play from:

1. K93
2. 962
3. 976
4. Q106

II. The opponents have reached a 4♠ contract, partner having overcalled in hearts. Partner leads the ♡A and dummy tables:

♠ A J 3 2
♡ Q 8 5
◊ A 7 4
♣ K 5 3

What would you play from:

1. 107
2. KJ94
3. J942
4. 1074

III.

♠ Q J 5 4
♡ A
◊ K 6 5
♣ J 9 7 5 3

♠ K 7
♡ K 10 8 5 2
◊ Q J 7
♣ 8 6 2

The opponents reached 3 NT and you led the ♡5. Declarer won in dummy and led a low spade to his 10. You won the king. What do you lead now if:

1. At trick one, partner played the nine and declarer played the three?
2. At trick one, partner played the three and declarer played the seven?

IV.   ♠ K 6 4
             ♡ K 6 3
             ◊ 8 6 4 3
             ♣ Q 8 6

                              ♠ 7
               ♡ A Q 9 8 4
                              ◊ 9 5 2
                              ♣ J 7 3 2

South opened 1♠, North raised to 2♠. South went on to 4♠. Your partner, West, led the ◊Q.

1. Which diamond do you play to trick one?
2. Which diamond would you play if you had nothing in hearts, but ◊K95?
3. Declarer wins the first trick with the ◊K and plays a trump to the king and a trump back toward his hand. What would you discard?

SOLUTIONS TO QUIZ ON DEFENSIVE SIGNALS:

I. 1. 9   (encouraging)
    2. 2   (discouraging)
    3. 6   (discouraging)
    4. 10 (encouraging)
II. 1. 10 (encouraging, hoping to ruff the third heart)
    2. 9   (encouraging)
    3. 2   (discouraging)
    4. 4   (discouraging)
III. 1. the ♡2
     2. the ◊Q
IV. 1. 2   (discouraging)
    2. 9   (encouraging)
    3. the ♡9, to show strength in that suit.

RESPONDER'S REBID:

This can be the most critical bid in the auction. Since OPENER'S REBID will often announce his high-card strength and suggest more about his distribution, RESPONDER may have a good idea what contract is best. Remember that when one player limits his values, as opener may do with his rebid, the other player becomes "captain." Therefore, the following principle is often applied to RESPONDER'S REBID:

> AT RESPONDER'S SECOND TURN, HE WILL OFTEN FIND HIMSELF "CAPTAIN." HE WILL BID AS HIGH AS HE FEELS IT IS SAFE TO GO, TRYING TO PLACE THE CONTRACT OR SUGGEST A CONTRACT. HE MAY SHOW WEAKNESS, DISPLAY INTEREST IN GAME OR BID GAME. OCCASIONALLY RESPONDER MAY TEMPORIZE WITH A (FORCING) BID IN A NEW SUIT, HOPING TO GET FURTHER INFORMATION.

Here is a table of responder's options at his turn to rebid. *This table assumes that opener has made a minimum rebid* at his second turn. If opener's rebid shows EXTRA STRENGTH, responder needs correspondingly LESS strength to bid again.

RESPONDER WILL FREQUENTLY BE THE "CAPTAIN" OF THE PARTNERSHIP.

WITH WEAKNESS (6-9 points):	PASS if you are satisfied to play right where you are. TAKE A PREFERENCE to OPENER'S first suit. REBID YOUR OWN SUIT CHEAPLY with a six-card suit or longer. BID 1 NT with a balanced hand and no liking for any suit.
WITH INVITATIONAL VALUES (10-12 points):	RAISE partner's second suit (with four-card support or better). RAISE his first suit if he rebid it, or RERAISE in your own suit (if partner raised you.) TAKE A JUMP PREFERENCE to opener's first suit. JUMP REBID IN YOUR OWN SUIT with a good six-card suit or longer. BID 2 NT.
WITH GAME-GOING VALUES (13 points or slightly more):	JUMP TO GAME in one of partner's suits, in your own suit, or in notrump. BID A NEW SUIT, forcing opener to describe his hand *more* fully.

There are a couple of situations that cannot be handled by our guiding principle.

IF OPENER'S REBID SHOWS *EXTRA* STRENGTH, RESPONDER NEEDS CORRESPONDINGLY *LESS* STRENGTH TO BID AGAIN. RESPONDER MAY BE ABLE TO BID GAME WITH AS FEW AS *8* POINTS. SLAM IS POSSIBLE IF RESPONDER HAS AN OPENING BID OPPOSITE OPENER'S EXTRA STRENGTH.

SOMETIMES *RESPONDER* WILL *LIMIT* HIS HAND EARLY. FROM THEN ON, HE WILL ACCEPT OR REJECT GAME TRIES BY OPENER; SHOW A SUIT HE HAD TO SUPPRESS EARLIER, PREFER ONE OF OPENER'S SUITS; OR MAKE A FURTHER DESCRIPTIVE BID.

QUIZ ON RESPONDER'S REBID:

I. *Opener* *Responder*
    1 ◇   1 ♡
    2 ♣

1. ♠ x x x
    ♡ A Q x x
    ◇ x x
    ♣ x x x x

2. ♠ x x x
    ♡ A Q x x
    ◇ x x x x
    ♣ x x

3. ♠ x x x
    ♡ A Q x x x x
    ◇ Q x
    ♣ x x

4. ♠ A x x x
    ♡ K Q x x x
    ◇ x
    ♣ A x x

5. ♠ K Q x x
    ♡ A Q x x
    ◇ x x
    ♣ x x

6. ♠ x x x
    ♡ A Q x x
    ◇ x x
    ♣ K Q x x

7. ♠ x x x
   ♡ A Q x x
   ◇ K Q x x
   ♣ x x

8. ♠ x x
   ♡ K Q J x x x
   ◇ A x
   ♣ J x x

9. ♠ K Q x
   ♡ A Q x x
   ◇ Q x x
   ♣ J x x

10. ♠ x x x
    ♡ A K x x
    ◇ x x
    ♣ A K J x

II. *Opener*   *Responder*
    1♠   1 NT
    2◇

1. ♠ x
   ♡ A Q x x
   ◇ J x x x
   ♣ x x x x

2. ♠ J x
   ♡ x x x x
   ◇ J x
   ♣ A Q x x x

3. ♠ x
   ♡ K Q 10 x x x
   ◇ J x
   ♣ J x x x

4. ♠ x
   ♡ A x x x
   ◇ K x x x x
   ♣ J x x

5. ♠ Q x
   ♡ Q 10 x x
   ◇ J x
   ♣ A 10 x x x

III. *Opener*   *Responder*
     1♡   1♠
     2♡

1. ♠ K Q x x
   ♡ x
   ◇ K x x x
   ♣ x x x x

2. ♠ A K x x x
   ♡ x x
   ◇ x x
   ♣ A K x x

60

3. ♠ A J x x x   4. ♠ A K x x x
    ♡ K Q x   ♡ x x
    ◊ J x x x   ◊ x x x
    ♣ x   ♣ A K x

5. ♠ K 10 x x
    ♡ Q x
    ◊ K x x
    ♣ Q J x x

IV. *Opener*   *Responder*
     1 ◊   1 ♡
     1 NT

1. ♠ K Q x x   2. ♠ K Q x x
    ♡ A J x x   ♡ A J x x
    ◊ K x x   ◊ J x
    ♣ x x   ♣ x x x

3. ♠ x   4. ♠ x
    ♡ K Q 10 x x x   ♡ K Q J 10 x x
    ◊ A x x   ◊ A Q x
    ♣ J x x   ♣ x x x

5. ♠ A x x x
    ♡ K Q x x x
    ◊ A x
    ♣ x x

V. *Opener*   *Responder*
     1 ◊   1 ♠
     2 ♠

1. ♠ Q x x x   2. ♠ K Q x x
    ♡ x x x   ♡ A x x
    ◊ K x x x   ◊ Q x
    ♣ Q x   ♣ x x x x

3. ♠ K Q x x x   4. ♠ J x x x
   ♡ A x   ♡ A J x
   ◊ K x x   ◊ x x x
   ♣ x x x   ♣ A K x

VI. *Opener*   *Responder*
   1♣   1◊
   1♡

1. ♠ K J x   2. ♠ x x x
   ♡ x x   ♡ x
   ◊ Q x x x x x   ◊ A J x x x
   ♣ J x x   ♣ Q x x x

3. ♠ x x   4. ♠ K Q x
   ♡ A J x x   ♡ J x
   ◊ K Q x x x   ◊ A K x x x
   ♣ J x   ♣ x x x

5. ♠ x x x
   ♡ x
   ◊ A K x x x
   ♣ K J x x

VII. Construct auctions for the following pairs of hands:

   Opener   *Responder*
1. ♠ K Q x   ♠ A x x x
   ♡ Q x   ♡ J x x x
   ◊ A J x x x   ◊ K Q
   ♣ Q x x   ♣ J x x

2. ♠ A Q x x   ♠ x x
   ♡ x x   ♡ A J x x x
   ◊ A K x x   ◊ Q x x x
   ♣ x x x   ♣ x x

3. ♠ x   ♠ K Q J x x x
    ♥ K x x   ♥ A J x
    ♦ A K x x x   ♦ x x
    ♣ Q J x x   ♣ x x

4. ♠ x x   ♠ A K x x
    ♥ K x x   ♥ A Q x x x
    ♦ A K J x x x   ♦ x x
    ♣ Q x   ♣ x x

5. ♠ x   ♠ A Q J x x
    ♥ K Q J x x x x   ♥ x x
    ♦ x x   ♦ A K x
    ♣ A J x   ♣ x x x

6. ♠ A K x x   ♠ x x x
    ♥ x x   ♥ K Q x x
    ♦ A K 10 x x   ♦ Q x
    ♣ K x   ♣ Q 10 x x

SOLUTIONS TO QUIZ ON RESPONDER'S REBID:

I.   1. Pass   II.   1.   Pass
      2. 2♦   2.   2♠
      3. 2♥   3.   2♥
      4. 2♣   4.   3♦
      5. 2 NT   5.   2 NT
      6. 3♣ (four-card support is preferred to raise opener's
           second suit.)
      7. 3♦
      8. 3♥
      9. 3 NT
     10. 4♣ or 5♣

III. 1. Pass
      2. 3♣
      3. 4♡
      4. 3♣. Invent a suit to
             temporize.
      5. 2 NT

IV. 1. 3 NT
     2. 2 NT
     3. 3♡
     4. 4♡
     5. 2♠

V.   1. Pass
     2. 3♠
     3. 4♠
     4. 3 NT

VI. 1. 1 NT
     2. 2♣
     3. 3♡
     4. 3 NT
     5. 3♣

VII. 1. 1♦ - 1♡
        1 NT - 2 NT
        3 NT - Pass

     4. 1♦ - 1♡
        2♦ - 2♠
        3♡ - 4♡
        Pass

     2. 1♦ - 1♡
        1♠ - 2♦
        Pass

     5. 1♡ - 1♠
        2♡ - 3♦
        3♡ - 4♡
        Pass

     3. 1♦ - 1♠
        2♣ - 3♠
        Pass

     6. 1♦ - 1♡
        1♠ - 1 NT
        2 NT - 3 NT
        Pass

REMEMBER YOUR
DEFENSIVE SIGNALS —
A HIGH CARD ENCOURAGES;
A LOW CARD DISCOURAGES.

Lesson 7

THINKING:
CHOOSING YOUR OPENING LEAD

In the last lesson, we saw possible strategies the defenders could apply. Among these were: *leading trumps* to deny declarer extra trump tricks; trying desperately to set up a fast trick or two with an *aggressive* lead; making a *safe* lead, expecting declarer to come up short of tricks in his contract, especially if given no help by the defense.

A good defender remembers that the opening lead is just the first step in his strategy. To make an effective opening lead, therefore, you must *use your imagination.* Visualize the dummy and imagine how declarer will probably play the hand. Then make the opening lead with the idea of countering his plans.

Here are some of your options in making the opening lead:

AGAINST NOTRUMP CONTRACTS:

Lead *your longest suit* if you think you can set up the long cards and regain the lead to cash them.

Lead a suit in which your partner *overcalled* (or opened the bidding). He is likely to have a good suit, plus entries.

Lead a suit in which you can *infer your partner has length.* To try to set up your partner's longest suit may be attractive if your hand contains few entries.

AGAINST SUIT CONTRACTS:

Lead a trump if the auction suggests that declarer may try to *ruff losers* in dummy.

Make an aggressive lead if dummy has advertised a *long, strong suit* that may provide declarer with *discards* for his losers. Leading from kings and queens and laying down aces are justified.

Make a passive, safe lead if dummy will be *weak*, without much help for declarer's losers. The defenders can afford to *wait* on their tricks. Several leads are passive:

1. the trump suit
2. a lead from a good sequence, especially ace-king
3. the first suit the dummy bid
4. a suit in which you have a worthless holding

Lead a singleton (or worthless doubleton), trying for a ruff, if *you have a weak hand* (so that partner is likely to have some high cards for entries). This lead is attractive if you have the ace or king of trumps to regain the lead before all trumps are drawn.

SUCCESSFUL LEADS AGAINST SUIT CONTRACTS REQUIRE CAREFUL THOUGHT AND A LITTLE LUCK.

QUIZ ON CHOOSING YOUR OPENING LEAD:

The bidding has been:

1. | *South* | *West* | *North* | *East* |
   |---------|--------|---------|--------|
   | | 1♠ | Pass | 2♡ |
   | Pass | 3♡ | Pass | 4♡ |
   | (All Pass) | | | |

Your hand, as South:

♠ Q 5 4
♡ 8 6 4
◊ K J 5
♣ J 9 6 4

2. | *South* | *West* | *North* | *East* |
   |---------|--------|---------|--------|
   | | | | 1♠ |
   | Pass | 2♠ | (All Pass) | |

♠ 8 5 3
♡ Q 9 5 3
◊ K 8 4
♣ J 9 3

3. | *South* | *West* | *North* | *East* |
   |---------|--------|---------|--------|
   | | | | 1♠ |
   | Pass | 3♠ | Pass | 4♠ |
   | (All Pass) | | | |

♠ J 6 4
♡ Q J 10 4 3
◊ A 8
♣ K 6 4

67

4. | South | West | North | East |
| --- | --- | --- | --- |
| | | | 1 ♡ |
| Pass | 1 ♠ | Pass | 2 ♡ |
| (All Pass) | | | |

♠ 7 5 3
♡ K Q 4
◊ K 5 3
♣ Q 9 5 3

5. | South | West | North | East |
| --- | --- | --- | --- |
| | | | 1 ◊ |
| Pass | 1 ♡ | Pass | 2 ♣ |
| (All Pass) | | | |

♠ K Q 6 4
♡ J 6 4
◊ A J 9 4
♣ 9 7

6. | South | West | North | East |
| --- | --- | --- | --- |
| | | | 1 NT |
| Pass | 3 NT | (All Pass) | |

♠ A K 7 5 3
♡ 8 6 4
◊ J 4
♣ 6 5 3

7.

South	West	North	East
			1 ◊
Pass	1 ♡	1 ♠	2 ◊
Pass	3 ◊	Pass	3 NT
(All Pass)			

♠ 9 4
♡ Q 7 4
◊ 7 6 5
♣ Q 10 7 5 2

8.

South	West	North	East
			1 NT
Pass	3 NT	(All Pass)	

♠ 10 9 4
♡ J 8 6 4
◊ 10 8 6 4 2
♣ 8

9.

South	West	North	East
			1 NT
Pass	2 ♣	Pass	2 ♠
Pass	4 ♠	(All Pass)	

♠ A 7 5
♡ K Q 10 4
◊ A 9 7 5 3
♣ 5

10. | South | West | North | East |
|---|---|---|---|
| | | | 1 ♡ |
| Pass | 4 ♡ | (All Pass) | |

♠ J 10 9 6 4
♡ A 7 5
◊ 5
♣ 10 6 4 2

SOLUTIONS TO QUIZ ON CHOOSING YOUR OPENING LEAD:

1. ◊ 5, hoping to get a *fast trick* or two before declarer establishes the spades for discards.
2. ♠ 3. Play *safe,* with dummy known to be weak.
3. ♡ Q, the normal *top-of-sequence* lead. This lead combines safety with a try at building a trick. Your hand is too strong to lay down the ◊ A. Partner is most unlikely to have the king.
4. ♠ 7. A *passive* lead, with dummy known to be weak.
5. ♣ 7. Dummy's most likely source of tricks is ruffing power on this auction, and you can tell declarer has losing diamonds to ruff since yours are strong.
6. ♠ 5. You must lead *low* here to keep communication with partner's hand, since you have no sure entry.
7. ♠ 9. *Lead your partner's suit.* He is likely to have a good suit for his overcall, plus entries.
8. ♠ 10, hoping to *find partner's long suit.*
9. ♡ K. You are too strong to lead your singleton club. Partner will probably never win a trick on this hand.
10. ◊ 5. You have a weak hand, so partner probably has an entry somewhere. Plus, you have trump control.

SLAM BIDDING THE EXPERT WAY:

Some slam bidding methods:

1. With *POWER*, as when partner opens 1 NT and you raise him to *6 NT* with a strong hand of your own.
2. With the *BLACKWOOD CONVENTION.* In many situations, a bid of *4 NT* is played as *ace-asking.* Partner replies as follows:

```
With no aces................5 ♣
With 1 ace ................5 ◇
With 2 aces................5 ♡
With 3 aces................5 ♠
With 4 aces................5 ♣
```

If your side has all the aces, you may continue with a bid of *5 NT,* which asks for *kings* and implies interest in a *grand* slam.

Remember that 4 NT is played as merely a *raise of notrump,* showing general interest in slam, if it is bid directly over a notrump opening or response. In most cases, a bid of 4 NT is *not* ace-asking unless a trump suit has been agreed on.

Note this well: THE TIME TO USE BLACKWOOD IS WHEN YOU KNOW THE POWER, GOOD TRUMPS AND CONTROLS NEEDED FOR SLAM ARE AVAILABLE, AND THE ONLY WORRY IS THAT TWO ACES MAY BE MISSING. BLACKWOOD IS NOT A SLAM-BIDDING TOOL, BUT A WAY TO AVOID SLAM WHEN A LACK OF ACES IS THE PROBLEM.

DO NOT, therefore, use Blackwood with shaky trumps, a void suit or a worthless holding in an unbid suit. Use it when *you* expect to *place the contract accurately* if you know *one* piece of information — *how many* aces your partner holds.

3. By CUEBIDDING. This is the method much preferred by better players:

> ONCE A TRUMP SUIT IS AGREED ON, A BID OF ANOTHER SUIT AT THE LEVEL OF GAME OR HIGHER SHOWS INTEREST IN SLAM AND PROMISES A CONTROL (most often, the *ace;* sometimes, especially later in the auction, a king or singleton or void). PARTNER IS INVITED TO BID A SLAM OR CUEBID A SUIT IN WHICH *HE* HOLDS A CONTROL. AFTER ONE OR MORE CUEBIDS, THE PARTNERSHIP DECIDES WHETHER TO BID SLAM.

CUEBIDDING is a superior method of slam bidding for several reasons:

1.   It is more *flexible. Either* partner may use his judgment and bid slam. In Blackwood, the 4 NT bidder must make all the decisions for his partnership.

2.   The partnership can show *where* its aces and kings are located.

3.   It is possible to show slam interest without getting as *high* as 4 NT.

An example of a CUEBIDDING auction:

Opener	Responder
♠ A Q 6 4	♠ K J 8 5 3
♡ 5	♡ J 7 3
◇ A K J 8 5	◇ Q 9
♣ J 6 4	♣ A Q 8
1 ◇	1 ♠
3 ♠	4 ♣ (1)
4 ◇ (2)	4 ♠ (3)
6 ♠ (4)	Pass

The partnership had this conversation:

(1) "I have a club control, probably the ace, and I think we may have a slam."
(2) "I have a diamond control, probably the ace, and you may be right."
(3) "We may have a slam, but I can't make any aggressive move at this point with losers in hearts."
(4) "If you need a heart control, I've got it."

The *first* cuebid you make normally shows *first*-round control — an ace (rarely, a void). A further cuebid of this same suit by either partner suggests *second*-round control, the king (rarely, a singleton).

You *cannot* begin to cuebid controls if there is doubt about what the trump suit will be, or when it is not even clear that your side is in the slam zone.

73

QUIZ ON SLAM BIDDING THE EXPERT WAY:

1. Partner opened 1 NT. What is your response with:

   ♠ A Q x
   ♡ K x x
   ♢ A Q x x x
   ♣ Q x

2. You opened 1♠, partner responded 3♠. What is your rebid with:

   (a) ♠ A Q x x x   (b) ♠ K Q J x x x
       ♡ A J x x   ♡ K Q x x
       ♢ A x   ♢ x
       ♣ K x   ♣ A x

   (c) ♠ A Q x x x   (d) ♠ K J x x x
       ♡ x x   ♡ x
       ♢ K x   ♢ A K J x x
       ♣ A K J x   ♣ x x

3. You opened 1♠, partner responded 3♠. With which of these hands would you now employ the Blackwood Convention?

   (a) ♠ A J x x x   (b) ♠ J x x x x
       ♡ K x x   ♡ A K Q x
       ♢ A x x   ♢ A Q x
       ♣ A x   ♣ x

   (c) ♠ A K x x x x   (d) ♠ A Q x x x
       ♡ x   ♡ A K
       ♢ A K J x   ♢ x x x
       ♣ K x   ♣ A x x

74

(e) ♠ A K x x x
♥ A J x x
♦ —
♣ K J x x

4. You opened 1♠, partner responded 3♠. What is your rebid with:

(a) ♠ A J x x x
♥ Q J x
♦ K x x
♣ A x

(b) ♠ K Q x x x
♥ x x
♦ A Q J x x
♣ x

(c) ♠ A Q x x x
♥ x x x
♦ A Q x
♣ A x

5. Partner opened 1♠, you responded 3♠, he bid 4♣. What do you bid now with:

(a) ♠ K Q x x
♥ x x x
♦ A Q x x
♣ K x

(b) ♠ K J x x
♥ A x x
♦ K J x
♣ J x x

6. Construct auctions for the following pairs of hands, using *cuebids* to reach a good slam or avoid a bad one.

Opener

(a) ♠ Q x x x
♥ A x x x
♦ x x
♣ A J x

Responder

♠ A K J x x
♥ x
♦ A K Q J x
♣ x x

(b)
  ♠ K x   ♠ A Q x x
  ♡ A J 10 x x   ♡ K Q x x
  ◇ J x x   ◇ Q x
  ♣ A K x   ♣ x x x

(c)
  ♠ K Q 10 x x   ♠ A x
  ♡ A x   ♡ x x
  ◇ J x   ◇ A Q x
  ♣ A Q x x   ♣ K J x x x x

(d)
  ♠ x x   ♠ A x
  ♡ Q x x   ♡ A K J x x x x
  ◇ A Q x   ◇ x x
  ♣ A Q x x x   ♣ K x

SOLUTIONS TO QUIZ ON SLAM BIDDING THE EXPERT WAY:

1. 6 NT
2a. 6♠
  b. 4 NT
  c. 4♣
  d. 4♠. No point in bidding 4◇, which would be a *cuebid*.
3. Only (c) is suitable for a Blackwood bid. With (a), you must be concerned about sufficient *power* for slam. With (b) the problem is a shaky *trump* holding. With (d), you have no *control* in diamonds. With (e), you have a void suit and need to know about *specific* aces.
4a. 4♠
  b. 4♠
  c. 4♣ or 4◇
5a. 4◇
  b. 4♠. Do not encourage slam by cuebidding the ♡A. Your hand is minimum for a forcing raise.

6a. | Opener | Responder |
|---|---|
| Pass | 1♠ |
| 3♠ | 4◊ (1) |
| 4♡ (2) | 5♠ (3) |
| 6♣ (4) | 7♠ |

(1) Control, slam interest.
(2) Control, slam interest.
(3) Clubs is the *only* problem.
(4) First-round club control.

6b. | Opener | Responder |
|---|---|
| 1♡ | 3♡ |
| 4♣ (1) | 4♡ (2) |
| Pass (3) | |

(1) Control, slam interest.
(2) I have a bad hand and I'm not willing to go past game to show the ♠A.
(3) I give up.

6c. | Opener | Responder |
|---|---|
| 1♠ | 2♣ |
| 4♣ | 4◊ (1) |
| 4♡ (1) | 4♠ (1) |
| 6♣ (2) | 7♣ (3) |

(1) Controls, slam interest.
(2) I'm willing.
(3) I have an *extra* club winner, so I'll shoot the moon.

6d. | Opener | Responder |
|---|---|
| 1♣ | 2♡ |
| 3♡ | 3♠ (1) |
| 4♣ (1) | 4♡ (2) |
| 5◊ (1) | 7♡ (3) |

(1) Controls, slam interest.
(2) I can't do any more with nothing in diamonds.
(3) It looks as if we have 'em all.

Lesson 8

THINKING: RECONSTRUCTING DECLARER'S HAND ON DEFENSE

As a defender, try to reconstruct declarer's holding ON EVERY HAND. It is impossible to produce best defense consistently if you do not. There are several things about declarer's hand you must try to learn:

(1) His high-card *points;* so you will know in what suits he is weak.
(2) His *distribution;* so you will know what suits are safe for the defenders to lead.
(3) His probable *tricks;* so you will know if you must hurry to get *your* tricks before it is too late.

The defenders should always try to count *their* potential *defensive tricks.*

The bidding will provide information about declarer's strength and pattern, and the opening lead may help. The defenders must also observe what high cards declarer plays and note as he shows out as suits are led. Try to get into the habit of *counting* declarer's hand as a defender. It will be well worth the effort.

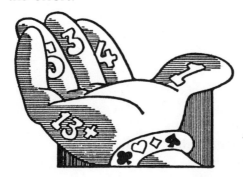

ALWAYS COUNT DECLARER'S HAND.

Here is a hand that illustrates the benefits of *counting* declarer's *distribution*.

```
              ♠ Q 5
              ♡ K 5
              ◇ Q J 7 4
              ♣ K 8 7 4 2
♠ 10 6 4 2          N
♡ J 9 4 2       W       E
◇ A 8              S
♣ Q 9 5
```

South	West	North	East
1 ♠	Pass	2 ♣	Pass
2 ◇	Pass	3 ◇	Pass
3 NT	(All Pass)		

You, West, lead the ♡2. Dummy plays low, and your partner wins the ♡A and returns a heart to the king. Declarer follows low to both heart tricks. Now declarer leads a diamond from dummy, playing the king from his hand. You win the ace.

You know declarer had at least nine cards in spades and diamonds combined (he would have opened 1 ◇ with four cards in each suit); and he has the ♡Q left in his hand, so he had at least three cards in that suit. Therefore, declarer had at most *one* club. You shift to the ♣Q (the queen is led in case declarer has the singleton jack), and you will make five tricks unless declarer has the ♣A. Declarer's hand is:

```
♠ A K J 9 3
♡ Q 10 7
◇ K 10 6 2
♣ J
```

QUIZ ON RECONSTRUCTING DECLARER'S HAND ON DEFENSE:

1.

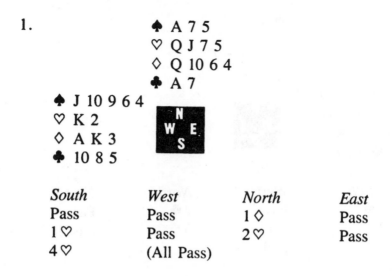

```
            ♠ A 7 5
            ♡ Q J 7 5
            ◊ Q 10 6 4
            ♣ A 7
♠ J 10 9 6 4
♡ K 2          N
◊ A K 3      W   E
♣ 10 8 5       S
```

South	West	North	East
Pass	Pass	1 ◊	Pass
1 ♡	Pass	2 ♡	Pass
4 ♡	(All Pass)		

You, West, lead the ♠J. Declarer wins dummy's ace, dropping the queen from his hand. The ♡Q is finessed to your king, and declarer ruffs your spade continuation. He draws another round of trumps, your partner playing the ten.

Next declarer plays the ♣AKQ and ruffs a fourth round of clubs in dummy. East plays the jack on the last round. Declarer ruffs another spade in his hand and leads a diamond toward dummy. What is declarer's distribution? What do you play on the diamond lead?

2.

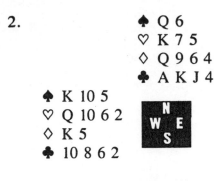

♠ Q 6
♥ K 7 5
♦ Q 9 6 4
♣ A K J 4

♠ K 10 5
♥ Q 10 6 2
♦ K 5
♣ 10 8 6 2

South	West	North	East
Pass	Pass	1 ♣	Pass
1 ♦	Pass	2 ♦	Pass
3 ♦	Pass	5 ♦	(All Pass)

You, West, lead the ♥2. Dummy plays low, partner plays the nine, and declarer wins the jack. Declarer leads the ♦A and a low diamond. You win and partner's jack falls. What do you lead now?

3.

♠ 10 8 3
♥ Q 9 7
♦ A Q J 10 4
♣ J 5

♠ K J 7 2
♥ A 5
♦ 7 6
♣ Q 9 8 4 2

South opened 1 NT, North raised to 3 NT. You, West, lead the ♣4. Dummy wins the jack, declarer following with the ten. Declarer now leads a heart to his king, and you win the ace. What should you lead at this point?

4.

	♠ Q 6		
	♡ A 9 4		
	◇ K J 6 4		
	♣ Q J 6 5		

♠ 8 7 4 3
♡ 5 3
◇ A 9 7 5
♣ K 9 2

```
     N
  W     E
     S
```

South	West	North	East
		1 ♣	Pass
1 ♠	Pass	1 NT	Pass
3 ♡	Pass	3 NT	Pass
4 ♡	(All Pass)		

You, West, lead the ◇ A, to which declarer follows low. What should you play at trick two?

SOLUTIONS TO QUIZ ON RECONSTRUCTING DECLARER'S HAND ON DEFENSE:

1. Declarer has one spade, four clubs and no more than five hearts; so he had three diamonds at least. You should *duck* the diamond lead. If declarer lacks the ◇ J, he will probably play dummy's ten and lose three diamond tricks. Notice that you must do your counting *in advance* on this hand so that when declarer leads a diamond, you can duck *smoothly* with your ace and king. A long hesitation will tell declarer that you have strong diamonds.

2. Lead a spade. Declarer failed to open the bidding and is known to have the ◇ A and the ♡ A and ♡ J. So partner should have the ♠ A.

3. Declarer is known to have the ♣ AK and the ♡ K, and he surely has the ◇ K too. If he needed to finesse in diamonds to set up the suit, he would do that *first*. So we know about *13* of declarer's high-card points. His spades,

82

therefore, cannot be as good as ace-queen. That would give him 19 points, too many for his 1 NT opening.

A spade shift must be safe, since partner must have one of the missing honors, and it is really the only chance for the defense. Declarer had five diamond tricks and three club tricks to begin with, and the ♡Q is now a winner. The contract will be made unless the defenders can cash the setting tricks in spades.

4. Lead a club. The bidding indicates that declarer has at least ten cards in hearts and spades; therefore, three or fewer cards in the minor suits. Even if you lead a club and find declarer with A-x, you lose nothing. He would discard his club loser on the ◊K anyway. But if *partner* has the ♣A, the defenders need to cash their club tricks right away, before declarer throws one of his club losers away on the ◊K.

BALANCING

> WHEN THE OPPONENTS STOP BIDDING LOW, ESPECIALLY WHEN THEY FIND A REASONABLE TRUMP SUIT, YOU SHOULD CONSIDER BACKING INTO THE AUCTION EVEN IF YOU WERE NOT STRONG ENOUGH TO ACT EARLIER. IT IS LOSING TACTICS TO LET THE OPPONENTS PLAY COMFORTABLY AT THE ONE OR TWO LEVEL. A BALANCING BID OR TAKEOUT DOUBLE MAY GET YOUR SIDE TO A MAKABLE CONTRACT OR DRIVE THE OPPONENTS TO A LEVEL WHERE YOU CAN SET THEM.

WHEN YOUR PARTNER BALANCES, REMEMBER THAT HE TOOK A CHANCE, *COUNTING ON YOU* FOR SUBSTANTIAL VALUES. DO *NOT* COMPETE FURTHER, TRY FOR GAME, DOUBLE THE OPPONENTS, OR TAKE ANY AGGRESSIVE ACTION UNLESS YOU HAVE EXTRA HIGH-CARD STRENGTH OR UNUSUALLY GOOD DISTRIBUTION. WITH AN AVERAGE HAND, DO NOTHING TO PUNISH PARTNER FOR HIS ENTERPRISE IN BALANCING.

DO NOT BALANCE WHEN:

1. Your hand is *extremely* weak.
2. You have a strong holding in the opponents' suit.
3. The opponents may be better off in some *other* suit.
4. The opponents stop bidding at a low level, but the auction suggests that they do *not* have a fit.
5. In a close case, you have values in the opponents' suit that will be useless if your side declares the hand.

If the opponents bid: 1 ♣ - 2 ♣ , or 1 ◇ - 2 ◇ , you will probably balance about 75% of the time. You will also balance more often than not when they open in a major suit, raise to two and stop there.

Another common balancing situation is when an opening bid on your left is passed around to you. This table lists the possible actions that are available and how their requirements compare to the same action taken in the *direct* position.

Action	Balancing (Passout) Seat	Direct Seat
Overcall	Less than an opening bid, as few as 7 HCP.	About an opening bid, perhaps more.
Jump overcall	Good six- or seven-card suit, about an opening bid in high cards. *Intermediate.*	Good suit, poor high-card strength. *Preemptive.*
1 NT	10-14 HCP, balanced pattern, usually a stopper in the opponent's suit.	16-18 HCP, balanced pattern, always a stopper in the opponent's suit.
Takeout double	8-9 HCP or more.	Close to an opening bid or more in high cards.
Cuebid	A freakish one- or two-suiter that will produce the tricks for game. May lack great high-card and defensive strength.	A hand that would have opened with a forcing two-bid. Great defensive and playing strength.

QUIZ ON BALANCING:

I. Your right-hand opponent opened 1 ♡, left-hand opponent raised to 2 ♡, passed around to you. How many high-card points would you expect partner to hold if your hand were:

(a) ♠ K x x
    ♡ x x x
    ◇ K x x x
    ♣ J x x

(b) ♠ A J x x
    ♡ J x
    ◇ A x x x
    ♣ Q x x

II. Your right-hand opponent opened 1 ♠, left-hand opponent raised to 2 ♠, passed around to you. What action do you take with these hands:

(a) ♠ x x
    ♡ A x x x
    ◇ K x x x
    ♣ Q x x

(b) ♠ J x x
    ♡ K x x
    ◇ A x x x
    ♣ K x x

(c) ♠ K J x
    ♡ Q x x
    ◇ A x x x
    ♣ Q x x

(d) ♠ A x x
    ♡ Q x x x
    ◇ A Q x x
    ♣ J x

(e) ♠ Q J 10 x
    ♡ K x x x
    ◇ A x x
    ♣ J x

(f) ♠ x x x
    ♡ K Q 10 x x
    ◇ A J 10
    ♣ x x

(g) ♠ J x x
    ♡ x
    ◇ Q J x x x x
    ♣ K J x

(h) ♠ x x x x
    ♡ x x
    ◇ J x
    ♣ A K x x x

86

III. Your left-hand opponent opened 1 ◊, passed around to you. What action do you take with these hands:

(a) ♠ A J x
    ♡ K x x x x
    ◊ x x
    ♣ x x x

(b) ♠ A x x
    ♡ Q x
    ◊ x x x
    ♣ K J x x x

(c) ♠ K J x x
    ♡ Q x x
    ◊ x x
    ♣ K x x x

(d) ♠ A K x x x
    ♡ A x x
    ◊ x x
    ♣ A J x

(e) ♠ x x x
    ♡ A Q x
    ◊ A Q x
    ♣ K J x x

(f) ♠ K J x
    ♡ A x x
    ◊ x x x
    ♣ J x x x

(g) ♠ A x
    ♡ K Q J x x x
    ◊ A x x
    ♣ x x

(h) ♠ x x x
    ♡ Q x x
    ◊ A J x
    ♣ K J x x

(i) ♠ A K x x
    ♡ A Q x x
    ◊ x x
    ♣ K x x

(j) ♠ K Q x x x
    ♡ A Q x x x x
    ◊ —
    ♣ Q x

(k) ♠ x x x
    ♡ A x x
    ◊ J x
    ♣ J x x x x

(l) ♠ x
    ♡ J x x x
    ◊ A J 10 x
    ♣ Q x x x

IV. The bidding has proceeded:

East	South	West	North
		1 ♡	Pass
2 ♡	Pass	Pass	2 ♠
Pass	Pass	3 ♡	Pass
Pass	?		

As South, with neither side vulnerable, what action do you take with these hands:

(a)   ♠ A x x   (b)   ♠ A Q x
      ♡ Q J 9 x   ♡ J x x
      ◊ Q x x   ◊ K x x x x
      ♣ x x x   ♣ Q x

(c)   ♠ A J x x
      ♡ x
      ◊ A x x x
      ♣ J x x x

V. Which of the following auctions by the opponents suggest that you balance?

(a)   1 ♡ - 1 ♠   (b)   1 ♡ - 1 NT
      2 ♡ - Pass   Pass

(c)   1 ◊ - 2 ◊   (d)   1 ♡ - 1 ♠
      Pass   2 ♠ - Pass

(e)   1 ♣ - 1 ♡   (f)   1 NT - Pass
      2 ♣ - 2 ♡
      Pass

(g)   1 ♡ - 1 NT   (h)   1 ◊   - 1 ♠
      2 ♣ - 2 ♡   1 NT - Pass
      Pass

(i)   1♡ - 1♠
     2♣ - Pass

VI. What action do you take in these situations as South?

(a)

East	South	West	North
1♡	Pass	1 NT	Pass
Pass	??		

♠ K x
♡ A x x x
◇ K 10 x x
♣ A x x

(b)

East	South	West	North
		3♡	Pass
Pass	??		

♠ K Q x x
♡ x
◇ A x x x
♣ K x x x

(c)

East	South	West	North
1◇	Pass	1 NT	Pass
Pass	??		

♠ x x
♡ K x x
◇ J x x
♣ A Q x x x

(d)

East	South	West	North
		1♣	Pass
2♣	Pass	3♣	Pass
Pass	??		

♠ A J x x
♡ K J x x x
◊ x
♣ x x x

(e)

East	South	West	North
		Pass	Pass
1♡	Pass	1♠	Pass
Pass	??		

♠ x x x
♡ K 10 x
◊ K Q J x
♣ Q 10 x

(f)

East	South	West	North
		1◊	Pass
1♠	Pass	2♠	Pass
Pass	??		

♠ x x
♡ K J x x
◊ A x x
♣ J x x x

SOLUTIONS TO QUIZ ON BALANCING:

I.   (a)   10-14 HCP.
     (b)   5-9 HCP.

II.   (a)   Double.
     (b)   Pass. Too risky to balance.
     (c)   Pass.
     (d)   Double.
     (e)   Pass.
     (f)   3♡.
     (g)   3◇.
     (h)   3♣.

III.   (a)   1♡.
     (b)   2♣ or 1 NT.
     (c)   Double.
     (d)   Double first, then bid spades.
     (e)   Double, then bid notrump.
     (f)   Double (a minimum).
     (g)   2♡.
     (h)   1 NT.
     (i)   Double and bid further.
     (j)   2◇.
     (k)   Pass.
     (l)   Pass.

IV.   (a)   Pass.
     (b)   Pass.
     (c)   3♠. You have more than partner can reasonably expect.

V.   (a)   Perhaps with a very suitable hand.
     (b)   No.
     (c)   Yes.
     (d)   Yes.
     (e)   No.
     (f)   No.
     (g)   No. If responder had true heart support, he would have raised to begin with.

(h) No.

(i) No.

VI. (a) Pass. If your heart intermediates were better, you might risk a double, which partner might be able to pass for penalties.

(b) Double. You would need more to double in the direct seat, but this is enough in the balancing position.

(c) Pass. West must have clubs since he did not raise diamonds or bid a major suit.

(d) Double. Partner should have a few points and shortness in clubs, therefore length in at least one of the majors.

(e) 1 NT. Don't worry about the spades. Partner is likely to have a stopper, and even if he does not, you will not be hurt badly at the one level.

(f) Double. Takeout for the unbid suits. This auction suggests you balance.

TRY TO RELAX WHEN YOU'RE DUMMY.

Lesson 9

THINKING: CONCENTRATION

Perhaps as much as 50% of your success at bridge depends on your ability to *keep your mind on the game*. If you aren't paying close attention, crucial details may escape your notice. Most of the mistakes an expert player makes are lapses in concentration, which he *knows* enough to avoid. The difference between the expert and the average player, however, is that the expert keeps his avoidable errors to a minimum.

Some ways to *help improve your concentration* at the bridge table:

1. Save your mental energy by *relaxing between hands*.
2. Do not follow *partner's* dummy play like a hawk if he is declarer. Let your mind rest.
3. Don't spend too much time on the *easiest* hands.
4. Don't wear yourself out trying to solve a "problem" that is really a complete *guess*.
5. Play in *tournaments*, which offer you extra incentive to concentrate.
6. Play for a small *stake* in social games.
7. *Study hands* that demand attention to details.

QUIZ ON AVOIDING HASTY PLAY:

All of these problems are easy, especially when presented in a problem setting when you're on the lookout for a catch. But they might well cause you trouble at the table if you *lost your concentration* and played too *hastily*. Studying such problems is a good way to train yourself to concentrate. How would you play these hands as declarer?

1. ♠ 7 6 4
   ♡ A J 9 7 5
   ◇ 3 2
   ♣ K Q 2

   ♠ A K 3 2
   ♡ K Q 10 8 4 2
   ◇ K 8
   ♣ 4

   Contract: 4♡
   Opening lead: ♣J

2. ♠ K J 9
   ♡ A 4 3
   ◇ 4 3
   ♣ A 8 7 6 5

   ♠ A Q 10 8 6 5 4
   ♡ 2
   ◇ K 5
   ♣ K 4 3

   Contract: 5♠
   Opening lead: ♡K

3. ♠ A 6 4
   ♡ 6 4
   ◇ A K Q 3
   ♣ 9 8 6 4

   ♠ Q 7 2
   ♡ K 5
   ◇ 8 7 6
   ♣ A K Q 5 2

   Contract: 3 NT
   Opening lead: ♠J

4. ♠ 10 9 2
   ♡ Q 10 7
   ◇ K 5
   ♣ A Q 10 6 4

   ♠ A 5
   ♡ A K J 8 6 4
   ◇ 6 3
   ♣ J 9 3

   Contract: 4♡
   Opening lead: ♠3 —
   right-hand opponent
   plays the queen.

5. ♠ A 6   6.   ♠ 10 3
    ♡ 10 7 5   ♡ J 10 7
    ◊ Q 10 6 5   ◊ Q 5 2
    ♣ A Q 4 3   ♣ K J 10 8 6

    ♠ Q 8 4   ♠ A K 4
    ♡ A 8   ♡ A K 9 8
    ◊ A J 8 4 3 2   ◊ A 8 4 3
    ♣ K 2   ♣ Q 9

    Contract: 3 NT   Contract: 3 NT
    Opening lead: ♠5   Opening lead: ♡4 —
                        right-hand opponent
                        plays low.

SOLUTIONS TO QUIZ ON AVOIDING HASTY PLAY:

1. Play *low* from dummy on the opening lead. You will take a *ruffing finesse* against East's ace later and establish a discard for one of your diamonds. This way, East never gets in to lead a diamond through your king. (If East *overtakes* with the ace at trick one, you get two discards and can avoid a spade loser.)

2. You must *duck* the opening lead. Later you will *discard a club* on the ♡A and establish the clubs by ruffing. In this way, you avoid the possibility that East might win a club trick and lead a diamond through your king.

3. Play the ♠*A* and lead the ♣*9* to your ace, beginning to unblock the suit.

4. You must *duck* the first trick to make sure that *West* can never win a spade trick later and lead through the ◊ K.

5. Play the ♠*A* and finesse in diamonds. Even if you lose the finesse, you are safe from another spade play. If you duck the first trick and East wins, a heart shift might set you.

95

6. Win the first trick with the ♡A and knock out the ♣A. With two *small* hearts left in your hand, and the jack and ten in dummy, you have a sure entry to the clubs.

STRONG AND WEAK TWO-BIDS; PREEMPTIVE OPENINGS

I. Opening bids of TWO OF A SUIT have traditionally shown hands with which opener expects to make a game regardless of what responder has. The requirements are:

---

1. Enough certain PLAYING TRICKS to make game.
2. At least 4 QUICK TRICKS.

Note that a certain number of *high-card points* is *not* a requirement.

Since opener states that game is certain, *responder must not pass.* You *must* respond, even with a worthless hand. Remember that opener bid *two,* not one, to make sure you would *not* pass with weakness.

After a strong two-bid, the auction must not die until game is reached. In responding, your options are:

---

1. 2 NT, which shows *weakness,* fewer than 7 high-card points.
2. A JUMP TO GAME IN PARTNER'S SUIT, which shows a weak hand (with no side ace, king or singleton), but good trumps.

Any other response is *positive* and promises 7 or more high-card points. You would have responded to an opening bid of *one,* and a *slam* is possible.

> 3. A SINGLE RAISE OF PARTNER'S SUIT shows 7+ high-card points and support.
> 4. A NEW-SUIT BID shows 7+ high-card points and a reasonable suit.

II. Many players have now adopted WEAK TWO-BIDS, which allow them to enter the auction more often. What type of two-bids you play is a matter for partnership discussion. The requirements for a WEAK TWO-BID are:

> 1. A GOOD SIX-CARD SUIT.
> 2. From 6 to 9 or 10 HIGH-CARD POINTS. Typically most of your high-card strength will be *in the suit you bid.*
> 3. At least 1 but no more than 2 QUICK TRICKS.

Avoid a WEAK TWO-BID if you have a *second suit* or a side-suit *void, or if your hand might make a better dummy* for other suit contracts than a declaring hand in your own suit.

> In responding to a WEAK two-bid, there are several options:
>
> 1. A NEW SUIT is *forcing* and asks opener to show support, rebid his own suit if it is especially strong, or bid another suit in which he has a high card.
> 2. 2 NT is forcing and (as most pairs play) asks opener to show an ace or king in another suit.
> 3. A SINGLE RAISE is an additional preempt. Responder is *not* trying for game, and opener may *not* bid again.
> 4. A RAISE TO GAME may be bid to make or it may be purely preemptive.

WEAK TWO-BIDS are played in spades, hearts and diamonds ONLY. A *2♣* opening is reserved for *all* strong hands, *regardless of what suit opener has*. His later bidding tells what kind of strong hand he has. The requirements for a 2♣ opening are the same as for any strong two-bid.

There are slight changes in the responses to 2♣:

1.	2◇ is the negative response, showing weakness.
2.	2 NT shows a balanced hand with 7+ high-card points.

If you play WEAK TWO-BIDS, you can use an *improved* system of showing balanced hands:

Open one of a suit and jump in notrump next	19-20 high-card points
Open 2 NT	21-22
Open 2♣ and bid 2 NT next ..	23-24
Open 2♣ and bid 3 NT next ..	25-26
Open 3 NT	27-28

III. Opening bids of three or more are *preemptive,* designed to *crowd the opponents* out of bidding space and prevent them from exchanging information and bidding accurately. *The time to preempt is:*

1.	When you have a hand that offers little *defense* against an opposing game or slam.
2.	When you hold a long, strong suit (typically, *seven* cards when you preempt at the three level, *eight or nine* if you preempt at an even higher level) that you can rely on for tricks, but *only* if your suit is trumps.
3.	When the vulnerability is in your favor.

In responding to a preempt, think in terms of your QUICK TRICKS, *not* your point count. Queens and jacks may be of no use to partner. If partner opens 3♠ with both sides vulnerable, you can expect him to have six or seven *winners,*

98

so you can raise to game with three or four QUICK TRICKS. Do not bid notrump unless you have a fit with partner and can expect to run his suit.

QUIZ ON STRONG TWO-BIDS:

I. Playing strong two-bids, what do you call as dealer with:

1. ♠ A Q J 10 x x   2.   ♠ K J x x x
    ♡ A K Q x   ♡ K J x x x
    ◊ A x   ◊ A K
    ♣ x   ♣ A

3. ♠ A Q x   4.   ♠ A K J 10 x
    ♡ A J x   ♡ A x
    ◊ A J x x x   ◊ A K Q x x
    ♣ A K   ♣ Q

5. ♠ A x
    ♡ A K x
    ◊ x
    ♣ A K J x x x x

II. Partner opens 2♡ (strong). What do you respond with:

1. ♠ Q J x x x x   2.   ♠ A Q x x
    ♡ x x   ♡ K x x
    ◊ x x x   ◊ x x
    ♣ x x   ♣ x x x x

3. ♠ x x   4.   ♠ x x
    ♡ J x x x   ♡ K Q x x
    ◊ x x x   ◊ x x x
    ♣ x x x x   ♣ x x x x

5. ♠ x x x
   ♡ x
   ◇ A x x x
   ♣ A J x x x

QUIZ ON WEAK TWO-BIDS:

III. Playing weak two-bids, what do you call as dealer with:

1. ♠ J 10 x x x x   2. ♠ x
   ♡ A x   ♡ K Q 10 x x x
   ◇ K x x   ◇ K J x
   ♣ x x   ♣ x x x

3. ♠ A Q J x x x   4. ♠ A x x x x x
   ♡ x   ♡ K x x
   ◇ Q J x   ◇ x
   ♣ x x x   ♣ Q J x

5. ♠ A 10 x x x x
   ♡ K x
   ◇ A x x
   ♣ x x

IV. Partner opens 2♡ (weak). What do you respond with:

1. ♠ A J x x   2. ♠ A K x x
   ♡ x x   ♡ J x
   ◇ A J x x   ◇ A K J x
   ♣ Q J x   ♣ x x x

3. ♠ K J x x   4. ♠ x x
   ♡ K x   ♡ A x
   ◇ A K Q x   ◇ A x x x x
   ♣ x x x   ♣ J x x x

100

5. ♠ x
   ♥ K J x x
   ♦ K J x x x
   ♣ J x x

V. Playing weak two-bids, what do you call as dealer with:

1. ♠ A K Q 10 x x   2. ♠ A K x
   ♥ A x   ♥ K x x
   ♦ A K x x   ♦ A Q x x
   ♣ x   ♣ A K x

3. ♠ A J x x   4. ♠ x
   ♥ x   ♥ K x x
   ♦ A K Q x   ♦ x x x
   ♣ A Q x x   ♣ K Q J x x x

5. ♠ A x
   ♥ A K x
   ♦ A K J x x x x
   ♣ x

VI. Playing weak two-bids, partner opens 2♣. What do you respond with:

1. ♠ x x x   2. ♠ x x
   ♥ x x x   ♥ A x x
   ♦ x x x   ♦ K Q x x x
   ♣ x x x x   ♣ x x x

3. ♠ Q x x   4. ♠ Q J x x x x
   ♥ K x x   ♥ x x
   ♦ Q J x   ♦ x x x
   ♣ J x x x   ♣ J x

5. ♠ A Q J x x
   ♥ x x
   ♦ x x
   ♣ J x x x

QUIZ ON PREEMPTIVE OPENINGS:

VII. With neither side vulnerable, what do you call as dealer with:

1. ♠ K Q J x x x x   2. ♠ x
   ♥ x x   ♥ Q J 10 x x x x
   ♦ J x x   ♦ Q J x
   ♣ x   ♣ x x

3. ♠ A 10 x x x x x   4. ♠ A Q J x x x x
   ♥ J x   ♥ Q x
   ♦ K x   ♦ K x x
   ♣ Q x   ♣ x

5. ♠ K Q J x x x x x
   ♥ —
   ♦ Q x x
   ♣ x x

VIII. With neither side vulnerable, partner opens 3 ♠ as dealer. How do you respond with:

1. ♠ x   2. ♠ A x x
   ♥ A K x x   ♥ Q J x
   ♦ A x x x   ♦ Q J x
   ♣ A J x x   ♣ A Q x x

3.　♠ J x x
　　♡ x
　　♢ A x x x
　　♣ x x x x x

4.　♠ K x
　　♡ Q x x
　　♢ K Q x x
　　♣ K J x x

5.　♠ K x x
　　♡ x
　　♢ A K Q x x
　　♣ A J x x

SOLUTIONS TO QUIZZES:

I.　1.　2♠
　　2.　1♠
　　3.　2 NT
　　4.　2♠
　　5.　2♣

II.　1.　2 NT
　　2.　3♡
　　3.　2 NT
　　4.　4♡
　　5.　3♣

III.　1.　Pass
　　2.　2♡
　　3.　2♠
　　4.　Pass
　　5.　Pass or 1♠

IV. 1. Pass
   2. 4♡
   3. 2 NT, intending to bid 3 NT if partner has a high card in clubs.
   4. 3♡, an additional preempt to keep the opponents out of spades.
   5. 4♡, preemptive. The opponents can make at least 4♠

V. 1. 2♣
   2. 2♣, intending to rebid 2 NT to show 23-24 balanced.
   3. 1♣, not enough *tricks* to open 2♣.
   4. Pass
   5. 2♣

VI. 1. 2♢
   2. 3♢
   3. 2 NT
   4. 2♢
   5. 2♠

VII. 1. 3♠
   2. 3♡
   3. Pass. Too much potential defense to preempt.
   4. 1♠
   5. 4♠

VIII. 1. 4♠, to make.
   2. 3NT
   3. 4♠, preemptive
   4. Pass
   5. 4 NT, Blackwood

Lesson 10

THINKING:
CARD COMBINATIONS AS DECLARER

Knowing the correct way to handle certain common combinations of cards is an important skill. There are *different aspects* to correctly handling card combinations.

1. You may need to know the *best play* to win the *maximum* number of tricks available from a suit.

For instance, the best play for SIX tricks with:

A K 10 9 x x   J x

is a *first-round finesse* against the queen.

2. *Correct play may assure* that you make, or have a chance to make, the maximum number of tricks available.

For instance, with:

(LHO)
K Q 8 x x   J x x x
(RHO)

be careful to *lead the jack first* in case right-hand opponent holds A-10-9-x.

3. In some situations, you may need to insure a certain *minimum* number of tricks from a suit. A "safety" play is like an insurance policy. You may *give up* the best play for the *maximum* number of tricks available but you *guard against a* devastating *loss* of tricks.

For instance, if you need FOUR TRICKS from:

K x x   A J x x

lead low to the jack immediately, hoping for Q-x-x onside. But if you require only THREE tricks from this suit, *cash the ace and king* and then lead toward the jack.

This combination of plays will allow you to make three tricks whenever it is possible to do so. You guard against losing a finesse to the *doubleton* queen and the loss of another trick later.

QUIZ ON CARD COMBINATIONS AS DECLARER:

In each of the following card combinations, what is the best play for the number of tricks indicated? There may be more than one problem to each card combination. Assume that the bidding and play have given no useful information. Entries are plentiful.

1. A K 10 x x   FIVE tricks

   J x x x

2. A Q x x x   FIVE tricks,
                          FOUR tricks

   x x x x

3. A J 9 x x   FIVE tricks

   Q x x x x

4. A x x x   THREE tricks

   Q J x x

5. A 10 9 x   THREE tricks

    Q 8 x x

6. A J x x   THREE tricks,
                              TWO tricks

    10 x x x

7. A K 10   THREE tricks

    x x x

8. K 10 9 8   TWO tricks

    x x x x

9. Q 10 x   ONE trick

    x x x

10. A J 8   TWO tricks

    9 x x

11. A J x x   FOUR tricks,
                              THREE tricks

    K 9 x x

12. A Q 9   THREE tricks

    J x x

13. A K 9 x   THREE tricks

    J x

14. K 10 x x   THREE tricks

    Q 9 x x

15. A 10 x x x   FOUR tricks

    K 9 x x

16. K Q 10 9 x   FIVE tricks

    A x x x

17. K Q 9 x x   FIVE tricks

    A x x x

18. J 10 x x   FOUR tricks

    A 9 8 x x

19. A J 10 x x x   SIX tricks

    Q x

20. K J x   THREE tricks

    Q x x x

21. J x x   THREE tricks

    A K x x

22. K 10   FIVE tricks

    A Q x x x

23. K 10   FOUR tricks

    A Q 8 x

24. Q x x x   TWO tricks

    J x x x

25. Q x   TWO tricks

    K x x x

26. A K 9 x   FOUR tricks,
                            THREE tricks

    J x x x

27. A K Q 10   FOUR tricks

    x x

28. K Q x x x x x   SIX tricks,
                            FIVE tricks

    x

*LEARNING HOW TO PLAY
CARD COMBINATIONS WILL
PUT YOU ON THE
WINNING ROAD.*

29. ♠ x x x
    ♡ x x x
    ◇ x x x
    ♣ A J x x

    ♠ A K x
    ♡ A K x
    ◇ A x x
    ♣ K 9 x x

You are declarer with these cards. The opening lead is the ♠Q. How do you play if the contract is:

(a) 2 NT?
(b) 3 NT?

30. ♠ A J x x
    ♡ x
    ◇ K x x
    ♣ Q x x x x

    ♠ x
    ♡ K J 10 x x x x
    ◇ A x
    ♣ x x

You opened 4♡ as dealer and all passed. The opening lead is the ♠ 10 and you win dummy's ace. How do you play the trumps?

SOLUTIONS TO QUIZ ON CARD COMBINATIONS AS DECLARER:

1. Play the ace and king.
2. FIVE tricks — lead low to the queen.
   FOUR tricks — cash the ace and then lead toward the queen.
3. Lead the queen for a finesse in case left-hand opponent holds K-10-x.
4. Play the ace and lead low toward the queen-jack.
5. Lead the queen for a finesse. If it loses to the king, lead to the ten next.
6. THREE tricks — lead low to the jack. If it loses, play the ace next.
   TWO tricks — play the ace and lead toward the ten.
7. Lead low to the ten, hoping the queen and jack are both onside.

8. Lead low to the eight. If that loses to the queen or jack, lead low to the nine next.
9. Lead to the ten. If the ace or king wins on your right, lead to the queen next.
10. Lead low to the eight, hoping that left-hand opponent has the ten plus one of the other honors.
11. FOUR tricks — lead low to the jack.
    THREE tricks — lead the ace and low toward your hand, planning to play the nine if right-hand opponent follows low on the second round. If left-hand opponent can win this trick, the suit has split evenly. If right-hand opponent has a singleton, win the king on the second lead and lead back toward the jack. This safety play guards against Q-10-x-x with either opponent.
12. Lead the jack; if it is covered, finesse the nine.
13. Lead low to the jack. If that loses, lead to the nine next.
14. Play the opponent of your choice for the jack and finesse against him.
15. Lead toward dummy and, if left-hand opponent follows low, play the ten. If right-hand opponent can win this trick, the suit has split evenly. If left-hand opponent shows out on the first lead, win in dummy and lead back toward your hand, covering right-hand opponent's card.
16. Play the king first, in case either opponent has J-x-x-x.
17. Play the ace first, in case left-hand opponent has J-10-x-x.
18. Lead the jack for a finesse. If it loses, lead the ten and finesse again.
19. Lead *low* to the ten the first time, in case left-hand opponent has the singleton king.
20. Lead low to the king. If it holds, lead low to the jack. You gain if left-hand opponent has the doubleton ace.
21. Cash the ace and lead low to the jack.
22. Lead low to the ten.
23. Lead low to the ten.

111

24. TWO tricks — play the opponent of your choice for a doubleton ace or king. Make the first lead through him, and play low from both hands on the second lead.
25. Lead low to the queen. If it holds, play low cards from your hand on any further leads, hoping left-hand opponent has the doubleton or tripleton ace.
26. FOUR tricks — cash the ace and king.
    THREE tricks — cash the ace and lead toward the jack.
27. Cash the ace and then lead low to the ten.
28. SIX tricks — lead low to the king. If it holds, lead low from dummy, hoping that left-hand opponent had the doubleton ace.
    FIVE tricks — play low from both hands on the first lead, in case right-hand opponent has the singleton ace.
29. (a) Take the *safety play* for *three* club tricks. Lead to the ace and back to the nine.
    (b) Lead a club to the jack, hoping for *four* club tricks.
30. Lead a heart to your *king*. This is a guess in principle, but you will gain by playing the king if left-hand opponent has the singleton queen. If left-hand opponent has the singleton ace, you will always lose two tricks.

"LOOSE ENDS" IN THE BIDDING

I. LIGHT OPENINGS

Many players like to open the bidding on sub-minimum values in third position. They want to direct a lead and get in a mild preempt in anticipation of the opponents' bidding. Light openings may be effective provided certain conditions are met:

> You must still have the *two defensive tricks* that a normal opening suggests.
>
> You must be able to *pass any response* with no trouble.
>
> You must *desire the lead* of your suit.

Playing *weak two-bids* will allow you to bid on certain hands that you might otherwise have to pass in third seat.

Your holding in the major suits, *especially spades,* is the most important consideration in opening borderline hands in *fourth* seat.

II. PASSED-HAND RESPONSES

> The consideration here is that *partner is no longer forced to rebid* if you respond in a new suit. Therefore, *you may be dropped* in your response if partner has opened on a minimum or sub-minimum hand. If you are a passed hand, you will be *less* inclined to make a *temporizing* response when you have support for partner's suit.

Responses such as 2 NT or a double raise of partner's suit, which would originally have shown an opening bid or slightly more, now show a hand worth *just under* opening-bid strength.

A jump shift suggests that the hand has been improved by partner's opening and is now worth an opening bid in support of his suit.

III. "PSYCHIC" BIDDING

Some players occasionally try the strategy of bidding with little or nothing at all! Weak opponents may be intimidated and fail to bid an easy game or slam. Even experienced opponents may be confused by a "psych" and miss out on their best contract.

The problem with psychic bidding is obvious; you may fool your partner disastrously instead of fooling the opponents. Even if your psychic strategy is successful, you damage your partnership's confidence and trust.

Another drawback to frequent psyching is that this practice may give your pair an *unfair* edge in competition. If your partner has seen you "operate" several times, he will be on the alert for your psychics, while the opponents may have no idea that a psych is possible.

Psychic bids may get you a good result once in a while, but they are losing tactics in the long run. They are no way to get a reputation as a fine bridge player. It is better to earn a tag as a steady, dependable player who wins with good technique and a sound knowledge of the game.

IV. AFTER A 1 NT OVERCALL:

If your partner *overcalls* 1 NT, the meaning of some of your responses changes.

---

1. A *cuebid* of the opponent's suit is used as the *Stayman Convention*. A 2♣ response would be natural and a signoff, unless the opponent's suit is clubs.
2. A *jump response in a suit* is no longer forcing, but only *invitational* to game. To create a forcing situation, cuebid the opponent's suit.

It pays to be aggressive in trying for game after partner has overcalled 1 NT. Partner's values are well-placed *behind* the opening bidder's, and the play will be easier for him when the location of most of the missing high cards is known.

V. PREEMPTIVE OPENINGS IN FOURTH SEAT

After three passes, a preemptive opening no longer has its usual meaning. You would pass the hand out if you had little high-card strength. Therefore, a preemptive opening by fourth hand is *constructive*. It shows a long, strong suit with values on the side. Partner is invited to gamble 3 NT if he has a few bits and pieces. Meanwhile, your high-level opening will keep the opponents out of the auction if they also have good distribution and wish to compete.

QUIZ ON "LOOSE ENDS" IN THE BIDDING:

I.   You are in third position after two passes. What action do you take with these hands?

1. ♠ x x
    ♡ Q J x x x
    ◊ A J x
    ♣ Q J x

2. ♠ x
    ♡ Q 10 x x x
    ◊ K Q x
    ♣ A x x x

3. ♠ x x
    ♡ A x x
    ◊ A Q x
    ♣ J x x x x

4. ♠ A Q 10 x x
    ♡ J x x
    ◊ A x x
    ♣ x x

5. ♠ Q x x
    ♡ A K J x x
    ◊ J x x
    ♣ x x

6. ♠ J x x
    ♡ J x x
    ◊ K Q 10 x x
    ♣ A x

7. ♠ A K J x
    ♡ x x
    ◊ Q x x
    ♣ Q 10 x x

8. ♠ K Q J 10 x
    ♡ x
    ◊ K x x
    ♣ J x x x

9. ♠ x
♥ Q x x
♦ A x x x
♣ A x x x x

10. ♠ K Q J x x x
♥ x x
♦ A J x
♣ J x

II. Partner has opened 1 ♥ after two passes. Your right-hand opponent passes, and you must respond *as a passed hand.* What action do you take with these hands?

1. ♠ J x x x
♥ x x
♦ A J x x
♣ Q J x

2. ♠ A Q x x
♥ Q x
♦ x x
♣ K x x x x

3. ♠ A Q x
♥ x x
♦ K 10 x
♣ Q 10 x x x

4. ♠ x x
♥ A J x x
♦ A Q x x
♣ x x x

5. ♠ x x
♥ A Q x
♦ J x x x
♣ A x x x

6. ♠ x x
♥ K x x x
♦ A K J x x
♣ x x

7. ♠ x x x
♥ K x x
♦ K x x
♣ A x x x

8. ♠ A K x x x
♥ x
♦ K x x x
♣ J x x

9. ♠ J x x
♥ A x x
♦ Q 10 x x
♣ A J x

10. ♠ A x x
♥ x x x
♦ Q x
♣ K Q x x x

III. Your left-hand opponent opened 1 ♡ and partner overcalled 1 NT. What is your action with these hands?

1. ♠ K x x x
   ♡ x x
   ◊ J x
   ♣ A Q x x x

2. ♠ K x x x x x
   ♡ x x
   ◊ x x x
   ♣ x x

3. ♠ A x x
   ♡ x x
   ◊ x x
   ♣ K J x x x x

4. ♠ K x x
   ♡ A x
   ◊ J 10 x x x
   ♣ x x x

5. ♠ A x
   ♡ x
   ◊ K x x x
   ♣ A Q x x x x

IV. You are in fourth position after three passes. What action do you take with these hands?

1. ♠ x
   ♡ J x x
   ◊ A K J x x x x
   ♣ x x

2. ♠ Q x
   ♡ K x x
   ◊ x
   ♣ A K Q x x x x

3. ♠ A K J x x x x
   ♡ A x x
   ◊ Q x
   ♣ x

4. ♠ x
   ♡ A J x x x
   ◊ K J x
   ♣ Q x x x

5. ♠ A Q x x x
   ♡ A J x x
   ◊ Q x x
   ♣ x

SOLUTIONS TO QUIZ ON "LOOSE ENDS" IN THE BIDDING:

I.   1. Pass. You lack the defensive values to open.
      2. Pass. You cannot pass a 1♠ response comfortably.
      3. Pass. You don't want to suggest a club lead.
      4. 1♠
      5. 1♡
      6. 1◊
      7. 1♣,   since you plan to pass any response.
      8. 2♣,   if playing weak two-bids; otherwise, pass.
      9. Pass. Perhaps the hand will be passed out.
     10. 2♣,   if playing weak two-bids; otherwise, 1♠.

II.   1. 1 NT. You prefer a better suit to respond 1♠ *as a passed hand.*
      2. 2♣,   planning to bid 2♠ next.
      3. 2 NT
      4. 3♡
      5. 3♡.   Avoid a *temporizing* response if you are a passed hand.
      6. 3◊.   Partner's opening has improved your hand.
      7. 2♡   is probably your best response.
      8. 1♠
      9. 2 NT
     10. 2♣.   Risk a temporizing response with your bad hearts.

III.   1. 2♡,   Stayman.
      2. 2♠
      3. 3♣,   invitational to game.
      4. 3NT.   Be aggressive after a 1 NT *overcall.*
      5. 2♡,   then bid clubs as a forcing bid. You may have a slam.

IV. 1. Pass
     2. 3♣
     3. 1♠
     4. Pass,   without length in spades.
     5. 1♠

YOU HAVE REACHED THE FINISH LINE!

COMPREHENSIVE GLOSSARY

"ABOVE THE LINE": Scoring of points won for overtricks, penalties and bonuses.

ACTIVE DEFENSE: The defenders' approach when they are desperate for tricks because declarer threatens to get discards for his losers.

ASSUMPTION: Technique by which declarer or a defender bases his play on the premise that the contract can be made or set.

ATTITUDE: Defensive signal that shows like or dislike for a suit.

AVOIDANCE: Technique in play whereby a dangerous opponent is kept from gaining the lead.

AUCTION: See BIDDING.

BALANCED HAND: Hand containing no void suit or singleton, and no more than one doubleton.

BALANCING: Backing into the auction after the opponents have stopped low, counting on partner to hold some values.

"BELOW THE LINE": Scoring of points that count toward making a game.

BID: Call in the auction that promises to take a certain number of tricks in the play and suggests a suit as trumps (or suggests the play be at notrump).

BIDDING: The first phase of each hand of bridge, when the players on both sides have a chance to name the trump suit and suggest how many tricks they expect their side to win in the play.

120

BLACKWOOD:	A conventional bid of 4 NT that asks partner to reveal, through an artificial response, the number of aces he holds.
BOOK:	(1) The first six tricks won by declarer's side; (2) the number of tricks the defenders must win before they begin to score undertricks.
BROKEN SEQUENCE:	Sequence such as QJ9, which contains a gap between the middle and lowest of the three cards.
BROKEN SUIT:	Suit that contains no cards adjacent in rank.
BUSINESS DOUBLE:	Penalty double.
CALL:	Any action, including a pass, taken in the bidding.
CAPTAINCY:	The bidding principle whereby one partner is obliged to take responsibility for placing the contract once his partner's hand is limited in strength.
CARD SENSE:	An intangible quality that those skilled in card play seem to possess.
CHICAGO SCORING:	A type of scoring in which every deal is taken as a separate entity. There are no rubbers or partscores carried over to the next deal.
COME-ON:	An encouraging attitude signal.
COMPETITIVE BIDDING:	Auctions in which both sides bid.

CONSTRUCTIVE BIDDING:	Auctions in which one side tries to reach its best contract without interference.
CONTRACT:	The number of tricks the side that wins the auction undertakes to make.
CONTROL:	Holding that prevents the opponents from taking two fast tricks in that suit. An ace; king; or singleton or void, if some other suit is trumps.
CONVENTION:	A bid to which an artificial meaning is assigned.
CROSS-RUFF:	A play technique in which cards are trumped in both partnership hands alternately on several successive tricks.
CUEBID:	(1) A bid of an opponent's suit, intended to show great strength. (2) A bid of a suit in which a control is held, intended to facilitate slam investigation. (3) Any of several conventional cuebids, such as Michaels.
CUT:	The division of the pack into rough halves prior to the deal.
DEAL:	The distribution of the 52 cards, 13 to each player face down, that begins each hand of bridge.
DECLARER:	The player who tries to make the contract by using both his own and dummy's cards.
DEFENDERS:	The partnership that opposes declarer and tries to defeat the contract.

DISCARD:	A played card that is not of the suit led nor of the trump suit.
DOUBLE FINESSE:	A combination of plays in which declarer finesses against two missing honors.
DOUBLE SQUEEZE:	An advanced type of squeeze in which each defender is squeezed in turn.
DOUBLETON:	A holding of two cards in a suit.
DOUBLE:	A call generally intended to increase the penalty suffered by the opponents if their last bid becomes an unsuccessful contract.
DRAW TRUMPS:	Technique in which declarer leads trumps, forcing the opponents to follow suit, until their trumps are exhausted.
DROP:	Cause a missing high card to fall by playing a still higher card or cards.
DUMMY:	Declarer's partner. The term is also applied to the dummy's cards, placed face up on the table.
DUMMY REVERSAL:	Technique by which declarer makes extra tricks by ruffing several times in his own hand and ultimately drawing trumps with dummy's trump holding.
DUPLICATE BRIDGE:	A contest in which the same hands are played several times by different players, allowing for a comparison of results.
DUPLICATION OF VALUES:	The condition in which the high cards and distribution of the partnership hands are ill-suited to each other.
ECHO:	A high-low sequence of play used by a defender to signal attitude or count.

ENDPLAY:	Technique by which a trick is gained through deliberately giving an opponent the lead in a position where he has no safe exit.
ENTRY:	A card used as a means of gaining the lead.
EQUALS:	Cards that are adjacent in rank, or that become adjacent when the cards that separate them are played.
FALSE CARD:	A card played with intent to deceive.
FALSE PREFERENCE:	A preference offered without true support, typically with two cards.
FINESSE:	Maneuver by which it is hoped to win a trick with an intermediate card, by playing that card after one opponent has already played.
FIT:	A holding that suggests the suit will adequately serve as trumps.
FIVE-CARD MAJORS:	A bidding style in which an opening bid of 1♠ or 1♡ promises five or more cards.
FOLLOWING SUIT:	Each player's first obligation in the play, to play a card of the same suit that was led to the trick if possible.
FORCING BID:	A bid that compels partner to take further action.
FORCING DEFENSE:	The defenders' approach when they try to exhaust declarer of his trumps by repeatedly forcing him to ruff.

FORCING PASS:	Pass made over an opponent's bid, which compels partner to double the opponents or bid further.
FREE BID:	Bid made when the alternative would be to pass and allow partner the next opportunity to act. Typically based on sound values.
FREE RAISE:	Raise of partner's suit in competition. Not a significant term, since such a raise does *not* imply extra strength.
GAME:	(1) A unit of scoring, two of which comprise a rubber; a game is won by the first partnership to score 100 or more points below the line. (2) Any contract that will allow the partnership to score game if fulfilled.
GAME TRY:	A bid that suggests interest in game and asks partner to assess his values and make the final decision.
GERBER:	A conventional bid of 4 ♣ that asks partner to reveal, through an artificial response, the number of aces he holds.
GRAND SLAM FORCE:	A bid of 5 NT, when used to show interest in bidding a grand slam in the agreed trump suit provided partner holds certain honors in trumps.
HIGH-CARD POINT COUNT:	Method of hand evaluation in which a numerical value is assigned to each high honor.
HONOR:	Ace, king, queen, jack or ten.

HONORS:	Bonus available in the scoring for a holding of four or all five honors in the trump suit in the same hand; or, at notrump, all four aces in the same hand.
HOLD-UP:	Refusal to take a winner, often for purposes of disrupting the opponents' communication.
INFERENCE:	A conclusion logically deduced from evidence.
INFERENTIAL COUNT:	An assessment of the entire distribution of the concealed hands, based on evidence from the bidding and the early play.
INTERIOR SEQUENCE:	Holding such as KJ109x, in which the equals are accompanied by a higher honor.
INTERMEDIATES:	Cards that may become winners as the cards that outrank them are played.
INVITATIONAL BID:	Bid that asks partner to continue to game or slam with maximum values.
JORDAN:	The conventional understanding in which a jump to 2 NT by responder, after the opening bid is doubled for takeout, shows a limit raise in opener's suit.
JUMP OVERCALL:	A suit bid usually made (as the next bid) after an opponent has opened the bidding, but at a higher level than necessary.
JUMP SHIFT:	(1) A jump of one level in a new suit by opening bidder. (2) A jump of one level in a new suit by responder. Either action implies great strength.

LEG:	A fulfilled partscore, a step toward game.
LEAD:	The first card played to a trick.
LIMIT BID:	Bid that promises no more than a pre-agreed amount of high-card strength.
LIMIT RAISE:	Direct double raise of partner's opening one-bid that promises invitational values only.
LONG CARDS:	Low cards that become winners because they are the only cards of their suit that remain in play.
MAJOR SUITS:	Spades and hearts.
MATCHPOINT SCORING:	Type of scoring used in duplicate (tournament) bridge, in which several different results from an identical deal are compared.
MAXIMUM:	Holding the greatest possible values for one's previous bidding.
MINIMUM:	Holding the fewest possible values for one's previous bidding.
NEGATIVE RESPONSE:	Bid, often artificial, that denies good values; made in response to partner's forcing action.
NOTRUMP:	Strain in which the play is conducted with no trump suit. The highest card played of the suit that is led to a trick wins that trick.
OBLIGATORY FALSECARD:	Falsecard that will lead to a certain loss if not played.

OBLIGATORY FINESSE:	The handling of certain suit combinations in which declarer plays a low card from both hands, hoping his opponent will be forced to follow suit with a high honor.
OFFSIDE:	Unfavorably placed for a finesse to work.
ONSIDE:	Favorably placed for a finesse to work.
OPEN THE BIDDING:	To make the first bid in the auction.
OPENING LEAD:	The lead to the first trick, made by the defender to declarer's left.
OVERCALL:	Bid in a suit after the opponents have opened the bidding (but before partner has taken any action).
OVERTRICKS:	Tricks taken in excess of those bid.
PARTIAL:	A partscore.
PARTNERSHIP:	Two players working as a unit. Bridge is played by two competing partnerships. Partners sit opposite each other. Trust and cooperation between partners are important features of the game.
PARTSCORE:	A contract below the level of game. Successful partscores can accumulate toward scoring game.
PASS:	Call in the auction when the player does not wish to bid, double or redouble.
PASSED OUT:	Deal on which none of the four players bid. Calls for another deal.
PASSIVE DEFENSE:	Defenders' approach when dummy is short of winners and the defense can wait on its tricks.

128

PENALTY DOUBLE:	Double made for a larger penalty, in the expectation that the contract will fail.
PERCENTAGE PLAY:	Line of play that will succeed most often, determined on only a mathematical basis.
PLAIN SUIT:	Any suit other than trumps.
POINT COUNT:	The method of hand evaluation whereby a numerical value is assigned to the possible trick-taking features of a hand.
POSITIVE RESPONSE:	Response to partner's forcing opening that promises certain good values.
PREEMPTIVE BID:	Bid made not for constructive purposes but merely to crowd the opponents and make it hard for them to bid accurately.
PREFERENCE:	A bid that chooses between two possible strains partner has offered.
PREPARED BID:	An opening bid in a low-ranking suit (often, a suit of only three cards), made so that a higher-ranking suit will provide an easy, space-saving rebid.
PRIMARY VALUES:	Aces and kings.
PROPRIETIES:	That section of the Laws of Contract Bridge that deals with ethics and etiquette.
PSYCHIC BID:	A bluff bid, made on a non-existent suit or without values, intended to intimidate the opposition.

QUANTITATIVE SLAM (GAME) TRY:	Bid that asks partner to pass or bid on, based strictly on the number of high-card values he holds .
RAISE:	A bid in the same suit (or notrump) that partner has just bid, often confirming that suit as trumps.
REBID:	(1) Bid the same suit a second time. (2) Any bid chosen at one's second turn.
REDOUBLE:	Call available in the auction that doubles, in turn, points scored if the contract is played doubled.
RESPONDER:	Opening bidder's partner.
RESTRICTED CHOICE:	A mathematical concept, based on the opponents' possible play from a holding of several equal cards, that may be helpful in determining the play of certain suit combinations.
REVERSE:	(1) A rebid in a new suit, such that the level of the contract will be increased if partner shows a preference for the first suit. (2) To bid in such a way, thereby showing a strong hand.
REVOKE:	Failure to follow suit when holding a card of the suit led.
RUBBER:	Unit of scoring in bridge, won by the side to first make two games, and carrying a large bonus.
RUFF:	To trump.

RUFF-AND-DISCARD (RUFF-SLUFF):	The lead of a suit in which both declarer and dummy are void, allowing declarer to discard a loser from the hand of his choice while he ruffs in the other.
RULE OF 11:	Device, applicable if the lead is known to be fourth highest, that may be used to make judgments in the play. Subtract the rank of the spot led from 11. The remainder shows the number of higher cards held by the hands, other than leader's.
SACRIFICE:	A deliberate overbid, but one in which declarer expects to be penalized fewer points than the opponents would score if allowed to play their own contract.
SAFETY PLAY:	The handling of a combination of cards so as to insure against a devastating loss of tricks.
SECOND HAND:	(1) The next player to have a chance to bid after the dealer. (2) The player who plays immediately after a trick is led to.
SECONDARY VALUES:	Queens and jacks.
SEMI-BALANCED HAND:	Hand which is neither balanced nor unbalanced by definition. 2-2-4-5 or 2-2-3-6 pattern.
SEQUENCE:	Three or more cards adjacent in rank, the highest one of which is an honor.
SET:	To defeat the contract.
SHORT CLUB:	See PREPARED BID.

131

SHUTOUT BID:	A preemptive bid.
SIGNAL:	Any of several conventional understandings through which the defenders can give each other information by means of the card they play.
SIGNOFF:	Bid suggesting that partner pass.
SIMPLE SQUEEZE:	Type of squeeze in which a single opponent is squeezed.
SINGLETON:	A holding of only one card in a suit.
SLAM:	A contract for 12 or 13 tricks, carrying a bonus in the scoring.
SPOT CARD:	Card below the rank of an honor.
SQUEEZE:	Technique, most often used by declarer, in which a defender is forced to relinquish a winner no matter what card he chooses.
STANDARD AMERICAN:	The bidding system most commonly used in America; essentially, the Goren style, with gadgets and refinements added.
STOPPER:	A card or combination of cards that threatens to produce a trick in a suit.
STRIP:	Play a suit or suits so as to make it impossible for an opponent to lead that suit or lead it safely.
SUIT-PREFERENCE SIGNAL:	Defensive signal that bears no relation to its own suit but shows interest in another, specific suit.

SURROUNDING PLAY:	Maneuver in which a defender breaks a suit by leading a high card that is part of a near-sequential holding.
SYSTEM:	The total framework in which the partnership assigns well-defined meanings to its bids and bidding sequences.
TABLE PRESENCE:	The ability to draw inferences from the extraneous things that happen at the table.
TAKEOUT DOUBLE:	Double that requests partner not to pass but to choose a suit (or notrump) to play in.
TEMPORIZE:	Bid a suit (often, an unplayable suit), in the expectation of supporting partner's suit later. May be required if no immediate raise is appropriate.
TENACE:	An honor or combination of honors that will be most valuable if the holder is fourth hand to play; e.g., AQ, KJ.
THIRD HAND:	In the auction, dealer's partner. In the play, leader's partner.
THIRD-SEAT OPENING:	An opening bid after two passes that may be based on sub-minimum values. Often it is intended as mainly lead-directing and mildly preemptive.
THROW-IN:	See ENDPLAY.
TRAP PASS:	Pass made with substantial values, including strength in the opponent's suit, in the hope of making a successful penalty double later.

TREATMENT:	A particular way of assigning a natural meaning to a bid or sequence of bids.
TRICK:	Four cards played in sequence, one by each player at the table, going clockwise.
TRUMPS:	The suit determined in the bidding to be that of the contract.
TRUMP CONTROL:	Technique by which declarer makes possession of the trump suit work to his advantage, exhausting the opponents of their trumps so he can safely establish and cash other winners.
TRUMP COUP:	The advanced play by which declarer can avoid losing a trick to an outstanding trump honor by forcing a defender to ruff and be overruffed.
TRUMP ECHO:	The high-low sequence of play in the trump suit, used in defense to show an odd number of trumps.
TRUMP PROMOTION:	Defensive technique in which declarer is forced to either ruff low and be overruffed or ruff high at the later cost of a trump trick.
TRUMP SUPPORT:	Usually four or more cards in partner's suit. Under some circumstances, three or fewer cards.
UNBALANCED HAND:	Hand containing a void suit or singleton.
UNBLOCK:	Play by declarer or defenders so as to allow the uninterrupted run of a long suit by proper management of the smaller cards.

134

UNDERTRICKS: Tricks that declarer has bid but fails to take.

UPPERCUT: Defensive technique in which a defender ruffs in with a trump intermediate and declarer is obliged to weaken his trump holding by overruffing.

VOID: A suit in which no cards are held.

VULNERABILITY: Condition in the scoring, achieved when one game is won toward completion of the rubber.

WEAK TWO-BID: Modern treatment in which an opening bid of 2 ♠, 2 ♡ or 2 ◇ shows a good six-card suit and about an average hand in high cards.

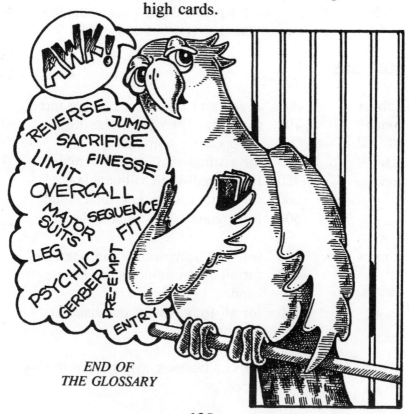

END OF
THE GLOSSARY

SCORING AT
RUBBER BRIDGE

TRICK SCORE — what you score for the tricks you bid and make as well as overtricks:

In spades/hearts	30 per trick
In clubs/diamonds	20 per trick
In notrump	40 for the first trick, 30 for every trick thereafter

If the contract is played *doubled* and made, multiply the usual trick score by two. If it is played *doubled and redoubled* and made, multiply the usual trick score by *four*.

To score *game,* you need 100 or more points in trick scores "below the line." The only points listed "below the line" are tricks scores for contracts that you bid and make.

BONUSES —

Rubber	500	if you win two games out of three.
bonus	700	if you win two games before the opponents win one.
Slam	500	for a small slam not vulnerable.
bonuses	750	for a small slam vulnerable.
	1000	for a grand slam not vulnerable.
	1500	for a grand slam vulnerable.
Honors	100	for four trump honors in one hand.
	150	for all five trump honors in one hand.
	150	for all four aces in one hand at notrump.
		(Honor bonuses may be claimed by a defender.)

For making a   50
doubled or
redoubled contract

For doubled	100	per trick doubled, not vulnerable.
and redoubled	200	per trick doubled, vulnerable.
overtricks	200	per trick redoubled, not vulnerable.
	400	per trick redoubled, vulnerable.

PENALTIES —what you score if you set the opponents' contract:

50	per trick, undoubled, not vulnerable.
100	per trick, undoubled, vulnerable.
100	for first trick . . .
200	for every trick thereafter, doubled, not vulnerable.
200	for first trick . . .
300	for every trick thereafter, doubled, vulnerable.

If redoubled, multiply the doubled penalty by two.

CHICAGO SCORING

CHICAGO scoring has supplanted rubber bridge scoring in many bridge clubs because of its simplicity and because of its close kinship to duplicate bridge scoring, with which many players are familiar. In CHICAGO, there are no rubbers or part-scores carried over to the next deal. Each deal stands alone and is scored separately.

In place of rubbers, a set of four deals, called a "chukker," is played. After each chukker, the players may swap partners for the next one, and the score for the chukker is tallied. The vulnerability for each of the four deals is pre-set. On the first deal, no one is vulnerable. On the second and third deals, the *dealer's* side is vulnerable. Both sides are vulnerable on the fourth deal. (The deal is passed around the table clockwise, as usual).

In the scoring, the bonuses for successful slams are the same, as are the penalties for setting an opposing contract. However, there are pre-set bonuses for making game and part-score contracts. In effect, these take the place of the rubber points earned at rubber bridge.

Bonus for a part-score: 50
Bonus for a non-vulnerable game: 300
Bonus for a vulnerable game: 500

In figuring your score for the deal, the trick score is added to the appropriate bonus.
Examples:

You play 1♡ and make three. You score 140: 90 for the trick score, 50 for the part-score bonus.

You play 4♠ (vulnerable) and make five. You score 650: 150 for the trick score, 500 for the vulnerable game bonus.

You play 5♣ (non-vulnerable) and make seven. You score 440: 140 for the tricks, 300 for the non-vulnerable game bonus.

You play 6 NT (vulnerable) and make six. You score 1440: 190 for the tricks, 500 for the vulnerable game bonus, 750 for the slam bonus.

A score sheet might look like this:

WE	THEY
140	
650	
440	
1440	
2670	

The score is generally rounded off to the nearest hundred. You would say, "We won a twenty-seven."

There are many possible variations of CHICAGO. The vulnerability scheme may be different; or you may decide to carry part-scores over to the next deal and award a bonus for .a partial unfulfilled after four deals.

139

WHAT THE PROPRIETIES ARE ABOUT:

In a game such as poker, all sorts of gamesmanship is allowed. In bridge, *skill in choosing a bid or play is emphasized.* A strict code of ethics and courtesy is part of the game. The better the players in the game, the higher the standard of ethics is likely to be. A higher standard of ethics is demanded in tournament play than in a social game at home. The purpose of the *Proprieties,* that section of the Laws of bridge that deals with conduct and ethics, is to make the game more enjoyable for everyone, no matter what the situation.

Please take time to read these excerpts from the Proprieties, excerpted from the *Laws of Duplicate Contract Bridge* (1975 edition). If you observe the principles set down here, you will find yourself respected as both a partner and an opponent.

CONDUCT AND ETIQUETTE

A player should maintain at all times a courteous attitude toward his partner and the opponents. He should carefully avoid any remark or action that might cause annoyance or embarrassment to another player, or that might interfere with another player's enjoyment of the game.

As a matter of courtesy, a player should refrain from:

Paying insufficient attention;

Making gratuitous comments during the play as to the auction or the adequacy of the contract;

Detaching a card from his hand before it is his turn to play;

Arranging the cards he has played to previous tricks in a disorderly manner or mixing his cards together before the result of the deal has been agreed to;

Making a questionable claim or concession; or

Prolonging the play unnecessarily.

It is a breach of the Proprieties to:

Use different designations for the same call ("A Club," "I'll bid a club," etc., are incorrect. "One club" is the only proper form).

Indicate any approval or disapproval of a call or play.

Indicate the expectation or intention of winning or losing a trick before play to that trick has been completed.

Comment or act during the auction or play to call attention to a significant incident thereof, or to the state of the score, or to the number of tricks that will be required for success.

Look intently at any other player during the auction or play, or at another player's hand for the purpose of seeing his cards or observing the place from which he draws a card.

Vary the normal tempo of bidding or play for the purpose of disconcerting the other players.

COMMUNICATIONS BETWEEN PARTNERS:

Communication between partners during the auction and play should be effected only by means of the calls and plays themselves. Calls should be made in a uniform tone without special emphasis or inflection, and without undue haste or hesitation. Plays should be made without emphasis, gesture or mannerism, and so far as possible, at a uniform rate.

It is improper for communication between partners to be effected through the *manner* in which calls and plays are made, through extraneous remarks or gestures, or through questions asked of the opponents or explanations given to them. When a player has available to him improper information from his partner's remark, question, explanation, gesture, mannerism, special emphasis, inflection, haste or hesitation, *he should carefully avoid taking any advantage that might accrue to his side.*

It is improper to have special understandings with partner regarding your bids and plays of which the opponents are unaware. The opponents are entitled to know about that fancy new bidding convention you and partner had decided to try out, and you are obliged to announce it to them before the game starts.

A NOTE ON PARTNERSHIP RAPPORT:

There are many bridge players who look on partner as a necessary evil, but your success at the bridge table will depend in great part on how well your partner performs. *Everything* that happens within your partnership can affect what kind of results you get, so your partner's morale should be important to you.

Nobody likes harsh criticism under any circumstances, but for people who play bridge seriously, the game is a real ego trip. We are sensitive about our game and our mistakes. If you point out your partner's errors right at the table (or, worse, if you are downright abusive), you won't accomplish anything constructive. On the contrary, you will probably get partner to dwell on his errors and induce him to play even worse.

A partnership at bridge is two people trying to act as one in an emotionally-charged setting. Recognize that when one player criticizes his partner, it is because he views partner's error as a direct reflection on his own ability; his ego has been ruffled.

You should always assume that your partner wants to win as badly as you do, and he is trying as hard as he can. Therefore, withold any criticism until after the game. Instead, you should be interested in *building* up his ego. If he makes an error, tell him that you would probably have done the same thing under the circumstances; or that he surely had what he thought was a good reason at the time he made his misguided bid or play.

Give his ego a chance to recover and he will play harder for the rest of the game.

Do your partner, your partnership and yourself a favor. Apply the Golden Rule when your partner makes an error.

AVOID CRITICIZING YOUR PARTNER.

DEVYN PRESS PUBLICATIONS
BRIDGE BOOKS

DISCARDED,